REFLECTING ON BUSINESS
A HANDBOOK OF CRITICAL THINKING

Linda M. Dyer

Concordia University

PEARSON

Custom
Publishing

Printed in Canada

10   9   8   7   6   5   4   3

ISBN 0-536-75333-7

BA 998439

LF

Please visit our web site at *www.pearsoncustom.com*

PEARSON CUSTOM PUBLISHING
75 Arlington Street, Suite 300, Boston, MA 02116
A Pearson Education Company

Table of Contents

Preface

This handbook is intended for use as a supplemental text in introductory, undergraduate business courses. It teaches students to bring a critical perspective to their reading in various fields of business–evaluating authors' arguments, uncovering key assumptions, analyzing why certain texts are more persuasive than others, and practicing related critical thinking skills. Each chapter contains the following elements: i) Expository text that discusses an aspect of critical thinking and shows why it is important to the process of evaluating ideas; ii) Worked examples of the critical thinking process applied to current as well as classic issues in business; iii) Brief sample texts that students can use to practice and develop their skills; iv) Exercises that encourage students to apply their skills and judgement to current business debates, and to read more widely in an area of their own interest.

I wish to thank a number of people who provided advice and encouragement in the preparation of this handbook. Olivia Rovinescu at the Centre for Teaching and Learning Services at Concordia University was generous in her support. Mick Carney, Nicole Bérubé and other business instructors made useful comments on early versions of the manuscript, and Patrizia Cacchione and Hélène Amram were among the student assistants who provided ideas and insights. I am grateful to Carol Acton who worked on the design and layout. Above all, I thank Charles Draimin who read and re-read successive drafts, offering constructive feedback and unflagging support.

1 What is critical thinking?

C ritical thinking is an approach to reading, thinking and learning that involves asking questions, examining our assumptions, and weighing the validity of arguments.

Sometimes questioning our beliefs about what we read comes naturally, but other times we may accept ideas and statements uncritically. Critical thinking can be developed as a frame of mind–a set of strategies that we will use as we determine whether or not to believe what we read or hear. In learning about critical thinking, we make these strategies explicit. If we can become aware of the activities of critical thinking, we will be able to use them consciously to think effectively and make intelligent decisions, both professionally and in our personal lives.

Critical thinkers are self-aware, curious and independent. They introspect on their own thinking processes, they work at knowing their own biases, and can name the strategies they are using when they make judgements (self-aware). They explore beneath the surface of issues, challenging ideas that originally seem to be obvious, trying out new approaches and seeking new viewpoints to extend their knowledge (curious). They listen to the ideas of others and learn from them, but then they use that learning to develop their own informed opinions, to understand the full range of their options, and to make their own judgements (independent).

"You're so critical!"

When we use the word *critical* in our ordinary conversations with acquaintances, we often mean negative or judgmental. Actually the word comes from the Greek word *kritikos* which means to question, analyse or make sense of something. This is the way we shall be using the term. Sometimes critical thinking will lead us to reject a conclusion; other times we will decide to accept an idea as valid. But in either case we will have subjected the issue to careful thought. So critical thinkers are not necessarily negative; rather, they try to assess the truth about a given matter.

Critical thinking about business

Many people claim that this is the age of information. We are bombarded with information when we watch television programs, read newspapers and explore the Internet. In recent times, information about the world of business often appears to hold centre stage. The dominant discourses are the productivity of companies, global markets, changing career paths, financial investments, consumer awareness, unemployment. This explosion of interest in business publications started during the 1980s and continues unabated today. It has been estimated that each year, $750 million worth of books about business are sold in the United States. In Canada the market is smaller, but the popularity of business books is also apparent on Canadian bookshelves. A 1996 survey conducted by the Canadian Publishers' Council estimated the size of the market for English-language business-related books at $40 million annually. This constituted 14% of the professional and reference books sold, and the relative market share of business books continues to grow. In addition, business magazines, seminars, workshops and consultant reports, all contribute to the burgeoning business literature with which managers and other interested parties must cope. Box 1-1 lists the top ten best-selling business books in North America in June 2003.

The sheer volume of this information can be intimidating; critical thinking skills can play a vital role in helping us to sift through the multitude of ideas. Simply asking: "Where have I heard this idea before?" helps us to deal with information overload. Critical thinkers recognise that the same idea can appear in radically different forms and they search for commonalities among diverse texts. They discard the terminological chaff and conserve the enduring kernels of truth in the current understanding of how businesses work.

Box 1-1: Best selling business books

This list of the top ten management books in North America, as of June 2003, comes from the web site of Books for Business, which claims to be the "world's largest business book store."

1. *Fish!: A Remarkable Way to Boost Morale and Improve Results*
   by Stephen C. Lundin et al (Hyperion)

2. *The Trusted Advisor*
   by David H. Maister (Touchstone)

3. *First Among Equals: How to Manage a Group of Professionals*
   by Patrick J. McKenna & David H. Maister (Free Press)

4. *Good to Great: Why Some Companies Make the Leap & Others Don't*
   by Jim Collins (Harper Collins)

5. *Execution: The Discipline of Getting Things Done*
   by Larry Bossidy & Ram Charan (Crown Business)

6. *Tomorrow's Gold: Asia's Age of Discovery*
   by Marc Faber (CLSA Books)

7. *New Financial Order: Risk in the Twenty-First Century*
   by Robert J. Shiller (Princeton University Press)

8. *Wall Street Meat: Jack Grubman, Frank Quattrone, Mary Meeker, Henry Blodget and me*
   by Andy Kessler (Escape Velocity Press)

9. *Never Say "No Comment"*
   by Ian Taylor & George Olds (LB Publishing)

10. *Why the Bottom Line Isn't: How to Build Value Through People and Organization*
    by Dave Ulrich & Norm Smallwood (John Wiley & Sons)

Reference http://www.booksforbusiness.com [Accessed 24 June 2003].

It is also said that this is the age of the expert. We count on experts to tell us how to look for a job, how to invest for our retirement, how to deal with difficult people at work, how to shop wisely. Our reliance on expertise extends beyond the normal sphere of the workplace; we're given expert advice on nutrition, keeping fit, gardening, raising children, caring for aging parents, etc. The problem is that, all too often, experts disagree. Their ideas contradict one another. "For every theory dragging companies one way, there are two other theories dragging it in another," complain John Micklethwait and Adrian Wooldridge, two vocal critics of the business literature. How do we decide what to believe? If the business experts were infallible there would be little need for critical thinking skills. But they are not. So we need to develop procedures we can use to assess the truth or validity of the differing ideas and conclusions the experts proffer.

Buyer beware

Many best-selling books written by business experts claim to deliver simple recipes for success that are based on a rich supply of anecdotes about successful executives and companies. They are often well-written, entertaining and optimistic in outlook. But *caveat emptor*–let the buyer beware. The ideas are not necessarily reliable, valid or scientifically sound. The popularity of the books may say more about the effectiveness of the authors' and publishers' marketing techniques, or about the insecurity of the managers who buy the books, than about the worthiness of the books' contents. In the words of business scholar, Larry Cummings, best-selling business books are "frequently among the most dangerous because they are so well done (that is, well done in a marketing and journalistic sense), and therefore they are easily read and so believable. They are likely to influence the naive, those who consume them without critically evaluating their content." A critical thinker does more than passively accept the ideas of others, even including the ideas of business experts.

As students of business, it is obvious that we need to think critically about the business discourse to improve our understanding of and performance in the world of commerce. Note, however, that critical thinking about business has a wider application. The values of business are permeating non-business spheres such as health care, politics, education and the world of art and culture. The spread of business values is sometimes explicit, sometimes implicit, sometimes almost surreptitious. Government representatives, university administrators, hospital directors, police chiefs, boards of artistic and community organizations, give voice to the pressure to revamp their activities to make them "run like a business." How valid is this generalization of business ideas to the not-for-profit sectors? What are the implications of extending the values of business into other spheres? It is important that we are able to ponder these issues, and so to understand and evaluate the major role that the world of business plays in all aspects of our lives.

The sponge

Many writers about thinking skills use the idea of a "sponge" to demonstrate a procedure we should avoid when reading or listening to others. A sponge, whether it is the underwater marine animal or the pad lying beside the kitchen sink, simply sits there and soaks up liquid. A reader who acts like a sponge simply soaks up information. Of course one does need to absorb knowledge about the world, particularly when you are learning about a new field. In your first marketing course, for example, you need to absorb the basics of marketing theory. Right now, you are "soaking up" some of the fundamentals of critical thinking. This is a necessary, though quite passive exercise. It is preliminary to the next step–evaluating and judging critically ideas in marketing or other fields of business. This is the stage we must try to attain. Being a critical thinker means going beyond the level of a passive sponge.

Dimensions of critical thinking

The critical thinking process can be divided into five major parts. First, critical thinking is purposeful–when we use these thinking strategies, we are trying to settle a problem, develop an answer to a question, or decide on appropriate action. It behooves us, therefore, to ensure that our thinking is directed at a significant and useful purpose and that we can state clearly the points at issue. This is the subject matter of the second chapter of this handbook in which we focus on the *central claims* of business texts.

A second dimension looks at the quality of the data and reasons that are available to support claims. Are there sufficient reasons provided? Is the information accurate? These and other questions that examine the *quality of the evidence* are presented in Chapter 3.

We also consider that claims and the evidence selected to support them are powerfully shaped by our basic assumptions or viewpoints. Can we identify the points of view that underlie the stated beliefs and evaluate their strengths and weaknesses? Can we turn our critical thinking focus onto our own *underlying assumptions and values*? Chapter 4 of the handbook looks at these notions.

Next we pay special attention to inferences about cause and effect. In the field of business, many claims suggest prescriptions and formulae such as: "If you do X in your firm, then Y will be the result," or "If employees are not given enough A, then they will become B." In Chapter 5 we will see that these are *causal claims* and we will address the complex issue of judging the validity of causal inferences.

The fifth dimension to be considered here is the way in which ideas are expressed in order to persuade readers and listeners. As critical thinkers, we must consider carefully the way in which key concepts are presented, how contradictory evidence is managed, and in general, how words can sway our judgements. These ideas are presented under the broad heading: *Techniques of persuasion*.

Consider an example
Let us now look at a brief text to which we might want to apply our critical thinking skills. There has been much concern recently about the underground economy, the notion that there are many transactions that occur among people who sell and buy goods and services "under the table" to avoid paying the applicable taxes. The following is a comment on the issue that we can evaluate critically:

> *"I'd pay my taxes," says Richard, a Montreal landscape gardener and snow-removal contractor, "but they are too high and I get so little for them. I used to give receipts and accept cheques; I charged and paid GST and PST, and I declared all my income. People would offer to pay me cash under the table to avoid the GST and PST but I said no. After a while, though, I asked myself what I was getting for all these taxes and decided that it really wasn't worth it. All these overpaid civil servants pushing paper until they get their fat, indexed pensions. All I get out of it is potholed roads, a failing health-care system, and giving welfare cheques to people who can but don't work. I have to scramble to get business and to satisfy difficult customers; and not even a good pension at the end. Anyway, I was losing customers to competitors who don't charge tax and probably don't declare their income either. I have food to buy for my family and Visa bills to pay. These things keep going up. I have no choice. I have to survive. If tax rates were lower, I'd pay my taxes and declare all my income. But the current set-up? No way!"*

> *Richard's views are not exceptional. According to research by the Fraser Institute, an economic think-tank, the underground economy now represents between 5 and 20 percent of GDP. It used to be smaller, but the expansion of small business and tax levels, and especially the introduction of the GST, over the last*

few decades have caused it to grow. Governments recognise this too. Lost taxation probably represents today something in the order of $30 to $40 billion to the federal and provincial governments. Governments' response is more stringent enforcement, as if this will solve the problem. But this misses the point. The answer is not heavy-handed enforcement of the tax act. It is expensive to hire government spies to chase down tax evaders. The answer, according to a director of the 70,000-member Canadian Taxpayers' Federation in Ottawa, is to reduce the tax burden to a level that people will judge to be fair. This will eliminate the incentive to cheat. High taxes force people to cheat. If taxes were lower, people would not resent complying.

As you read the text, several questions may occur to you as you decide whether or not the writer has made a good case for lowering taxes.

1. Is tax reduction better than enforcement? Will compliance really increase if taxes are reduced?

2. If compliance does increase, will this make up for the loss caused by a lower tax rate?

3. What is the effect of phrases like "pot-holed roads," "fat, indexed pensions" and "government spies?"

4. How relevant are Richard's household expenses to his argument that he should not pay taxes? In general, does the anecdote about Richard affect the persuasiveness of the author's conclusion?

5. Why does the author say that more stringent enforcement "misses the point?"

6. Who are the people who are likely to join the Canadian Taxpayers' Federation? What is the effect of noting that there are 70,000 members?

7. What do you think is the position of the author of this piece? In fact, who is the author and what is his/her background?

8. In your own opinion, what are the reasons that people evade taxes? Which, if any, of them are morally justified?

These are the types of questions a critical thinker raises. When you have applied your critical thinking skills to a piece like this, you may decide, in the end, to accept whole-heartedly the views of the author, to accept them cautiously and with specific reservations, to seek out further information before deciding one way or the other, or to reject the ideas outright. Whatever the outcome, you will have clearly-defined reasons for your position.

Critical thinking and effective communication
Another important outcome of developing your critical thinking skills is that you can improve your own arguments when you write or speak. You will know how to state your views clearly and provide appropriate justification for them. You will be able to avoid fallacies in reasoning, explore your own underlying assumptions, and deal effectively with evidence that runs counter to your views. In general, you will develop further your appreciation for the use of *language*. Careful attention to words can make our writing not only clearer, but more persuasive. Throughout our discussion of critical thinking skills, we will find that they translate quite neatly into guidelines for effective communication.

Resource material for additional reading:
Chaffee, J. (1998). *The thinker's way*, Little, Brown & Company.

Micklethwait, J. & Wooldridge, A. (1996). *The witchdoctors: Making sense of the management gurus*, Random House, page 16.

Pierce, J. & Newstrom, J. (1996). *The managers' bookshelf*, 4th edition. Harper Collins, New York. Interview with L. Cummings, page 22.

Rehner, J. (1994). *Practical strategies for critical thinking,* Houghton Mifflin Company.

Source material for examples and exercises
Canadian Publisher's Council, http://www.pubcouncil.ca/

Cordon, S. (1998) Tax cuts would foil underground economy, critics say, *Montreal Gazette*, 6 March, E3.

Lippert, O. & Walker, M. (1997). *The underground economy: Global evidence of its size and impact*, The Fraser Institute, Vancouver.

2 Claims

The first thing we must do if we are to evaluate an argument is to identify the author's *claim*. A claim is the major conclusion of a piece of writing that the author is trying to persuade you to accept. It is pointless to criticise a thesis if you are unable to say clearly what the author's claim is.

Sometimes, the central claim is explicitly stated and is easy to find. At other times, the job of finding the central claim is a greater challenge because it is implicit in the author's statements, that is, it is not stated outright. If the latter is true, you will have to state the claim in your own words. In a short article, the claim may appear at the very beginning of the piece. It sometimes appears in the title or as a headline of a newspaper article. The central claim may also be placed near the end of the article as a way of a conclusion.

Certain words or phrases may indicate that the author is about to state a claim. They include words such as *therefore, thus, in summary, I believe that, clearly, in short, the data show that, as a result, in fact,* and synonyms of these words. If you are having trouble finding the claim, it may be helpful to look for these *cue words*, read the phrases that immediately follow them, then decide which seems to be the main idea of the article. It is important to ensure that your statement of the claim is *fair*– that you have not distorted the author's meaning. After taking the time to evaluate a claim in depth, you don't want the author to respond: "Actually, you've missed my point. That's not what I said!"

Most of the other statements in the article will be *evidence,* the examples and reasoning that are presented to support the claim. We will discuss evidence in some detail in another section since it is normally on the basis of evidence that we decide whether or not to accept the claim. At this point, we simply note that a claim is not an example, a definition or a statistic. It is usually a broader issue, addressed at a greater level of abstraction than the evidence. For example, let's say that you read a passage that reports an anecdote about the case of a company that took a retailer to court for selling counterfeit versions of their trademark products. In the same passage is the statistic that an estimated 39% of the software in Canadian computers was not legally purchased. Neither of these pieces of information is the claim, rather, the claim is the more general statement that pirated merchandise is a big problem for manufacturing firms. The anecdote and statistic are evidence provided in support of the claim.

Uncontested claims

Given our focus on questioning and evaluation, we might wonder whether there are any situations where we might accept a claim without examining the evidence. Should we accept *any* claim without challenge? In fact, shouldn't we probe and question *all* the information that authors present? Let us reiterate, however, that critical thinking does not mean negative thinking. When we read or hear a claim, we may indeed decide to accept it as unproblematic. If we tried to question every single sentence that we read or heard, we would be paralysed. Here are some conditions in which people may accept a claim without challenge, even if no evidence is provided in its support.

1. We usually do not contest claims that are consistent with our own experiences and observations, things that we have actually seen, heard or touched: *The roads are congested with traffic between 4 and 6 pm.* Similarly, we accept claims that relate to subjective experiences: *I like the taste of black olives* or *Golf is my favourite sport.*

2. Some claims appear to be facts that are independent of interpretation—*Quebec is larger than Nova Scotia.* Events that happened are often not questioned, for example, when we read a newspaper report of a train accident or an announcement of a merger between two firms, we tend to accept this type of claim as true. These events are not uncommon and well within the realm of possibility.

3. Areas in which there is agreement among experts, or strongly-supported general claims that are common sense are often uncontested. Knowledgeable and

intelligent people are in general agreement that *You cannot be in two places at one time.* Business scholars agree that *Frederick Taylor has often been called the father of modern management.*

4. Technical or mathematical claims are usually accepted without challenge. We do not question that debits equal credits in double-entry accounting or that a 486 processor is slower than a Pentium 4 processor.

Of course, accepting something as unproblematic *now* does not mean that we must *always* continue to accept it as unproblematic. For example, even agreement among experts can be a transitory phenomenon. As new information arises, we are free to re-examine the situation and challenge claims which we no longer believe to be true. Box 2-1 presents an example of a once-unproblematic claim that was re-examined in later years.

Contestable claims

When a claim does not fall into one of the categories described above, we need to question its truth or falsity using our critical thinking strategies. Authors may present claims that are not commonly-accepted knowledge. For example, claims that *People who have excelled in the academic world make poor entrepreneurs* or that *Having a mandatory retirement age decreases a country's productivity and economic progress* are contestable claims. Political commentaries and editorials in the newspaper are a rich source of contestable claims. It is important to note that readers and listeners find contestable claims to be much more interesting and significant than claims that can stand without challenge. Contestable claims often introduce new ideas that awaken curiosity and cause people to think about things in new ways. If everything we read was an unproblematic claim, it would be dull reading indeed.

On occasion you may see a contestable claim presented as if it were a fact, as in: ***The fact is*** that close supervision is totally inappropriate in the modern workplace; or *There is **no doubt** that a sizeable reduction in taxes is necessary to stem the brain drain.* Simply labelling a claim as fact, however, or saying that it is beyond doubt, does not mean that it is an uncontested claim. Bosses, neophyte employees and "old-hand" employees may have very different reactions to the claim about close supervision. Economists, employers, job seekers and government officials may have varying opinions on the possible outcomes of tax reduction. Neither claim, then, is independent of interpretation. Unlike the examples in #2 above, they generally would be classified as contestable claims.

Box 2-1: An uncontested claim becomes problematic

Henri Fayol, a French industrialist, developed a profile of the manager in 1916. Managers, said Fayol, plan, organize, coordinate and control. Fayol's claim entered the general vocabulary of business and was accepted as unproblematic–his profile of managers was described in practically all introductory text books in business, and was routinely taught in business courses for undergraduates. There seemed to be general agreement among experts that this was an accurate characterization of managers.

Almost sixty years later, a challenge arose to Fayol's claim. Henry Mintzberg, a professor of management at McGill University, conducted a number of research studies in which he observed managers closely as they did their work. As a result, he published an article in the *Harvard Business Review* (1975) entitled, "The manager's job: folklore and fact." The article begins, "If you ask managers what they do, they will most likely tell you that they plan, organize, coordinate, and control. Then watch what they do. Don't be surprised if you can't relate what you see to these words (p. 163)." Mintzberg proposed that Fayol's classic claim was merely myth or folklore. His aim in this article was to "break the reader away from Fayol's words and introduce a more supportable and useful description of managerial work (p. 164)." Rather than being a systematic

---

When making contestable claims, authors must provide evidence to justify their positions, and our job as critical thinkers is to examine and evaluate the justification. The quality of the reasoning and evidence (which will be covered in the next section) is what leads us to accept or reject contestable claims. Contestable claims cannot stand on their own. Without evidence, discussing contestable claims will rapidly degenerate into "My opinion against yours." In a related vein, we frequently hear the notion that "Everybody's opinion is of equal value" or "I have a right to my own opinion." Subjective opinions do have their place, of course, but little progress will be made in understanding the business world and how it works if we fail to see the crucial difference between simply stating that something is true, and providing relevant and solid reasoning for our statements.

An example
Read the following passage and decide what the author's claim is.

and thoughtful planner, the manager has a job characterized by rapid pace, a variety of brief and discontinuous activities, and little time or inclination to reflect. Rather than planning broad strategies for the firm, based on aggregated, documented reports, managers prefer telephone calls, impromptu meetings, even hallway gossip.

Mintzberg made a new claim–that the manager's job was best described in a series of ten roles. These included interpersonal roles (such as figurehead and leader), informational roles (including the collection and dissemination of information) and decisional roles (such as entrepreneur and disturbance handler).

Challenging Fayol's claim certainly rang bells with many managers. In a retrospective commentary, Mintzberg reports that a common reaction to his article was "You make me feel so good. I thought all those other managers were planning, organizing, coordinating and controlling, while I was busy being interrupted, jumping from one issue to another, and trying to keep a lid on the chaos."

Mintzberg, H. (1990). The manager's job: Folklore and fact, *Harvard Business Review*, March/April, p. 163-176. The article first appeared in *Harvard Business Review*, July-August, 1975.

"Self-praise is no praise at all." This was one of my grandmother's maxims. It is not socially acceptable to brag about yourself and your accomplishments, she said. Ladies and gentlemen do not boast.

But Grandma did not live in today's competitive work environment. Modesty is worse than useless at a job interview when dozens of my fellow-students are vying for the job I want. I'd be a fool not to tell the recruiter about the excellent paper I wrote about Activity-Based Costing, and how much I've learned about his company by surfing the Internet. And after I get the job, if I don't tell my boss how well my project is going, or the great skills I'm picking up at night school, who will? How will she know that I'm the one deserving of the big year-end

> *bonus? Team-work is hot these days, and it's so easy to get lost*
> *in a crowd. I've got to let the right people know how many great*
> *ideas and long hours of work I contributed to the team effort.*
> *In short, it's a dog-eat-dog world, and if I want to get ahead,*
> *I've got to have the loudest bark.*

You should have noted the cue words, *in short,* at the end of the passage. The claim is not stated explicitly but the author's main point can be summarized as: "Self-praise is necessary for career advancement." An alternative wording could be: "Modesty is inappropriate in a competitive work environment," or "Bragging leads to success at work," or some similar formulation. It would not be appropriate to say that the claim was "It's a dog-eat-dog world," or "I've got to have the loudest bark," or even "Grandma was wrong." While these are colourful comments, they are not intelligible outside of the context of the passage, and none of them provides a good summary of the author's major point.

The rest of the paragraph contains the writer's reasoning and evidence presented in support of the claim.

Presenting claims

We have said that a good statement of the author's claim is the first step to evaluating it critically. When stating a claim, we try to present the essence of what the author is saying in an accurate and concise manner. Occasionally we can find a sentence or phrase in the author's own words that is a good statement of his or her claim; more often we must paraphrase and summarize elements of the text to state the claim clearly and efficiently.

While a claim is often stated as a sentence, especially when the text is short (like a newspaper article or the passage above), there are other ways of presenting claims. For longer texts, where a single sentence will not suffice, authors may provide a *list of important concepts* and a series of propositions about how these concepts are related. The claim may also be presented graphically as a diagram or drawing–a *concept map*. Concept maps are a compact way of summarizing complex material and can make the authors' claims very memorable. A picture, the saying goes, is worth a thousand words. Concept maps may be simple boxes-and-arrows figures that highlight the main issues and show relationships. They may look like tree diagrams, geographical maps, or other creative images that summarize the author's main point (see Box 2-2).

Writing effectively

Critical thinking about claims has implications for your own writing. Since a clear understanding of the claim is so important to readers, make sure that when you are the author you present your main ideas with clarity and emphasis. Put the claim near the beginning or end of your report, and use the cue words discussed above (e.g. *in conclusion, therefore, the data show that*) so that there can be no confusion as to what your claim is. The title of your text, and subheadings where necessary, should make your logic transparent to the reader. Make your titles work for you: As a heading, *Section Three* is much less useful than *Executive pay should be public knowledge*. In longer reports, you may find concept maps to be helpful in emphasizing your main points. Use pictures and other vivid images to make your claims clear and memorable for your readers.

Resource material for additional reading:

Booth, W., Coulomb, G. & Williams, J. (1995). *The craft of research*, University of Chicago Press.
Johnson, B. (1998). *Stirring up thinking*, Houghton Mifflin Co.

Box 2-2: Concept maps

The exercise of developing your own concept maps can help you to learn and remember the material you read for your courses. This is especially true when your concept maps contain images that are meaningful to you. In addition, concept maps can be an efficient and effective method of communicating the claims you make in your own reports to your readers.

Pictures have become more and more central to people's understanding of the world around them. Beginning in the mid-nineteenth century, the then-new technology of the photograph led to an explosion of reproductions of pictures and images in posters, advertisements, books, newspapers and later, television. The historian, Daniel Boorstin, has labelled this phenomenon the "Graphic Revolution." Some social observers believe that images are taking over from words as the primary medium of communication today.

We can conclude, then, that graphic representation of concepts and claims has become increasingly important for communication with the average reader. In fact, the cognitive processing needed to develop the concept map is an aid to our own understanding and memory.

Here are some tips to help you develop your own concept maps:

1. In making your concept map, start with a list of the main ideas to be represented. These may be headings or subheadings from the text. If headings are not provided, try to decide what words would be the most effective summary of each section of the text. It is important that you stick to single words or short phrases.

2. The structure of your map may be boxes and arrows, pictorial representations, time-lines, a tree-and-branch organization, overlapping circles, or a variety of other formats. You do not need to pick a structure in advance, just let it develop naturally as you proceed with your thinking about the concepts and the relationships among them.

3. Remember that your concept map may be highly individual—its evolution depends on the images, symbols and graphics that are most meaningful to you. You will find that certain conventions are intuitive—arrows, for example, usually denote cause and effect linkages; circles or other boundaries are used to group related ideas. You will develop your own conventions over time. Colour and shapes may be used judiciously, for instance, blue oval for advantages and red rectangle for disadvantages.

4. If you intend to use your concept map as an illustration in your own written report, make sure that it is well labelled and that the significance of the images you chose is clearly described in the text.

The strength of a concept map is its ability to summarize concisely large amounts of information. The concept map should never be more than one page. Having a few well-chosen words is much better than cluttering the map with excess words. Your goal is that a single glance will evoke ideas that may have been expressed in several pages of written information. This can be especially useful when you need to review material before an examination or oral presentation.

Boorstin, D. (1961). *The image*, Harper & Row Publishers, New York.

Exercise 2-1: Finding claims
Read each of the passages below and state the major claim being made by the author. What cues did you use to locate the claim? Is it a contestable claim?

1. The loyal employee is a creature who has become extinct. A recent survey from the Arthur Anderson group indicates that less than half the workforce in the industrial world will be holding full-time jobs by the beginning of the 21st century. Already in 1993, one out of three American workers had been with their employers for less than one year and almost two out of three had been at the same company for less than five years. The average person is now expected to hold as many as eleven different positions throughout his or her life. How did this sad state of affairs develop? First, there is the high demand, locally and internationally, for talented workers. Headhunters and competitive salaries encourage ambitious individuals to flit about from job to job. Secondly, today's organizations are highly unstable. The old adage, "Here today, gone tomorrow," applies. Consider a roster of the 100 largest US companies at the beginning of the 1990s. You'll find that only 16 are still in existence. During the decade of the 1980s a total of 230 companies, or 46%, disappeared from the Fortune 500 listing. Global competition and evolving technologies have forced firms to downsize or die. As a result, lifelong employment has faded away. Neither companies nor individuals can afford to cherish ideas about loyalty any more.

2. Professor Michael Howe of Exeter University in England has done substantive research on excellent performance in sport and in the arts. As a result of his studies, he and his colleagues believe that the notion of innate ability–what we call talent–is a myth. Rather success is determined by training, motivation and above all, long hours of practice. Professor Howe studied expert swimmers, tennis players, violinists, and so on, and found that thousands of hours of devoted practice was required for excellent performance, even among so-called "child prodigies." Many outstanding performers were not seen as particularly gifted as children, but training opportunities, encouragement and hard work paid off for them over time. The myth of talent persists only because we do not normally observe the lengthy, gruelling practice sessions engaged in by most experts. Professor Howe's findings have important lessons for teachers, parents and students alike.

3. Make way for the emergence of a new, powerful group of consumers–the tweenies. The tweenies, young people aged 9 to 14, account for 2.4 million of the Canadian population with a collective consumption power of 1.4 billion dollars. Realizing the potential sales volume that can be generated by these youngsters, marketers have focussed their advertising and promotional budgets on creating brand loyalty amongst them. Look at the advertising supplements in the newspapers. Look at the billboards. The average age of the models has been dropping like a rock. Tweenies now have sophisticated brand preferences despite their youth. They buy brand names

such as Adidas, Nike and Tommy Hilfiger. They enjoy vibrant, flashy apparel that draws attention. When interviewed about their clothing choices, these youngsters maintain that Tommy shirts and Adidas sweat-pants make them look "cool and mature." There can be little doubt that marketing to tweenies has been very successful and very lucrative for manufacturers and retailers in the fashion industry.

4. Bank employees used to have low-pressure, low-stress jobs, but with developments in telephone and electronic banking, all of that is changing. Workers at bank branches are no longer just tellers who carry out transactions; now most routine transactions are done automatically. The job of the branch banker has become focussed on learning about investment products, giving advice to customers, soliciting new business, and meeting sales targets to improve the bank's bottom line. And according to a study by the trade newspaper, *Investment Executive*, bankers are reporting that these new duties are causing levels of pressure and job stress to rise.

5. Testing consumer products on animals must stop. Animal tests are not accurate; data from them cannot be extrapolated to human beings. There are enormous differences in metabolism and physiology among rats, rabbits, dogs, pigs and human beings, so product tests on animals do not prove that the products are safe for human use. More than half of all the prescription drugs approved by the FDA (US) between 1976 and 1985 on the strength of animal tests caused side effects so serious that the drugs had to be re-labelled or removed from the market. Most cosmetic companies no longer conduct animal testing. New methods have been found so companies no longer have to kill or maim defenceless animals to conduct their research. Corporations that continue to use animal tests must be persuaded, by concerned citizens and ultimately by government legislation, to find alternate means of testing their products.

Exercise 2-2: Contestable and unproblematic claims
*Review the following claims and decide whether they are **contestable** or **unproblematic**. Which of the contestable claims are true in your opinion? Which do you believe are false? Why do you think so?*

1. Employment equity legislation has made salary discrimination a thing of the past.

2. Children should be protected from commercial advertising.

3. In the late 1990s, the Bank of Montreal and the Royal Bank proposed a merger.

4. The use of cross-functional teams increases the success rate of new product innovations.

5.   There won't be enough money in the Canada Pension Plan to allow young people to have a comfortable retirement when they turn 65.

6.   In 1998, expenditures of governments in Canada accounted for over a third of our gross national expenditure.

7.   Rewards motivate employees.

8.   In economics, equilibrium exists when supply equals demand.

9.   The glass ceiling syndrome is a primary reason why women leave large organizations and start their own businesses.

10.   Pollution from industrial waste has been a leading factor in environmental degradation and decline.

Exercise 2-3

In this week's newspapers or business magazines, find two contestable claims and two uncontested claims that are relevant to the world of business.

> You may want to look at the following publications both for this exercise and on a regular basis: Daily you will find very informative the *Globe and Mail's Report on Business* and the *Financial Post* section of the *National Post*; monthly there is *Canadian Business* magazine. (Regular subscribers to the *Globe and Mail* and the *Financial Post* also receive monthly magazines of the same name). In addition, local city newspapers have business sections. Important US business publications include the daily *Wall Street Journal* and the magazines, *Business Week, Forbes,* and *Fortune.* The weekly business and current events magazine, *The Economist,* published in Britain, is particularly good for international business news.

Exercise 2-4

Take your readings for one of your other courses this term. Are there *concept maps* presented to illustrate any of the issues? What changes could you make to *personalize* these concept maps so that they become more meaningful and memorable for you? If no concept maps are presented, make a list of the important concepts in the text and develop your own concept map.

3 Evidence

We have defined a *claim* as the central idea that the author of a piece is trying to persuade you to accept. An author who makes a claim usually offers reasons *why* you should accept it. *Evidence* is any statement that is a response to the question: Why is this true? It may consist of statistics, details of past events, anecdotes, written accounts, previously established claims, or other statements and reasoning that provide support for the claim. In the absence of evidence, a claim is merely unsubstantiated opinion; the more contestable or controversial the claim, the more important that it be bolstered by solid evidence.

Finding the evidence

Evidence helps us to form judgements about claims. Just as it is crucial to identify the claim, we must locate the evidence before we can evaluate an argument. An *argument* is the combination of a claim and the evidence for it. Note that this differs from the common use of the word "argument" to mean "disagreement or contention." In a longer piece of writing, there will be several arguments–claims and evidence– that the author presents. Certain *cue words* indicate that the author is about to present a piece of evidence. Look out for phrases like *because, as a result, in the first place, in the second place, for example, in addition, given that, studies show, for the following reasons,* and synonymous phrases. Read the following passage, and locate the claim and evidence provided. The sentences are numbered to aid our analysis.

Students today are more knowledgeable than they were a decade ago (1). In the first place, good early education plays an important role in this situation (2). Because of the prevalence of daycare, children leave home earlier, learning earlier to communicate with others and develop academic skills (3). For example, children in daycare are taught to read stories, write words and solve simple math problems even before they enter elementary school (4). In addition, teachers today are more highly educated than in the past (5). Most high school teachers hold at least a Bachelor degree, and most university teachers have PhDs (6). At all levels, people receive training in teaching during their degree programs (7). Compared with the past, therefore, teaching is more effective nowadays (8). Finally, advances in high technology provide students with a number of chances to expand their knowledge (9). I read in the newspaper that more than 50% of Canadian families have at least one personal computer at home (10). Nowadays, students can use the Internet to learn much more information about their courses or other interests in a convenient and efficient way (11). In summary, early education, better teachers and advancing technology have created more knowledgeable young people (12).

Here, the central claim, *Students are more knowledgeable than they were a decade ago*, is stated explicitly and appears both at the beginning and the end of the passage. Why does the author think this? Several pieces of evidence are provided to answer our *Why is this true?* question. Notice the cue words such as: *in the first place, for example, in addition* and *finally* which precede the evidence. The evidence offered has to do with early learning in daycare (sentences 2-4), the skills of teachers (sentences 5-8) and the availability of computers (sentences 9-11).

Notice that each piece of evidence has to be explained–in fact, each is treated like a subordinate claim which itself needs to be supported. The broad evidential statement about the availability of computers, for example, is supported by more detailed evidence about the prevalence of computers in Canadian households and the use of the Internet by students.

Quality of evidence

Of course, the mere presence of evidence is not automatic proof that the claim is acceptable. Evidence may be strong and substantial or weak and shaky. It is rare that we can be absolutely certain, beyond the shadow of doubt, about the evidence for any claim. Our job becomes one of evaluating whether the supporting evidence is of high quality and makes the claim highly probable, or whether it is of low quality, making the claim highly dubious. There are a number of ways in which we can test the quality of the evidence.

Accuracy

The first and most important characteristic of good evidence is its accuracy. Obviously, if you know that the information provided in justification is false, it undermines if not negates the claim. The problem is that accuracy can be impossible to judge without an independent and infallible source of information; usually we simply do not know whether the evidence provided is accurate. We could set out to verify the information by doing research of our own; more often we use *proxies* or other cues to decide whether the information is accurate. One such cue is whether or not the author makes other obvious errors. Even "trivial" errors like grammar and spelling mistakes, or inaccurate quotations, undermine confidence in the author's reliability and makes the argument less persuasive. Other cues that suggest accuracy relate to the precision of the evidence, and our judgement about the source of the information (see below).

Precision

Good evidence is appropriately precise. If we hear that a mutual fund made 18.4% last year, we are more convinced by this precise number than if we were told that it did "quite well" or even "almost 20%". Saying that the turnout at a sports event was "rather low" is less effective than saying that only 63 people attended (see Box 3-1). Overuse of ambiguous and abstract words such as *a great deal, many, often, a high probability, few, usually*, and so on is indicative of low precision. Using numbers, and providing direct quotations of what people actually said are the common ways of increasing the precision of our evidence. As we noted above, precision is sometimes used as a proxy for accuracy. Saying that 63 people attended suggests that we actually counted heads or ticket stubs, and creates the impression of accuracy.

On the other hand, it is possible to be too precise. Appropriate levels of precision vary in different fields. It would be absurd for an accountant who is filling in his time-sheet to say that he spent 17 hours, 9 minutes and 34.6 seconds on a particular project, though someone in the field of athletics, say, a sprinter might measure his running speed in hundredths of a second. A manufacturer would not list a product weight as 8.4162 kilograms; that level of precision might, on the other hand, be quite appropriate for an experimental chemist. Over-precision, like under-precision, can detract from the credibility of our evidence.

Box 3-1: Numbers and credibility

Isn't it odd that people are so impressed by numbers? Accountants, economists, psychologists and their ilk take ordinary events and behaviours, translate them into numbers–and then their descriptions seem to acquire a special mystique. Just because activities are expressed in a quantitative language, people find them more convincing than when they are stated in simple prose.

Why such faith in the power of numbers? It is difficult to say, but part of the explanation may be that numbers are commonly associated with science. According to philosopher Abraham Kaplan, our excessive regard for numbers is a legacy of the nineteenth century, when advances in measurement led to great strides being made in the physical sciences. Kaplan cites Lord Kelvin who wrote: "When you can measure what you are speaking about, and express it in numbers, you know something about it; but when you cannot measure it, when you cannot express it in numbers, your knowledge is of a meagre and unsatisfactory kind." Quantitative measurement–numbers–in this view is the essence of scientific progress. Still today, as in the 19th century, science is generally believed to be the key to understanding the truth about our world, and thus the basis for improvements in human life and endeavours.

Kaplan, A. (1963). *The conduct of inquiry*, Harper & Row Publishers, Inc.

Sufficiency

To be persuasive, an author must present sufficient evidence to support a claim. In the field of business, it is unlikely that any claim can be substantiated by a single piece of data. If you had a single personal experience with a rude bank-teller last week, this incident alone would not be sufficient to support the claim that customer service in the banks has deteriorated markedly. Just how much evidence is sufficient, however, varies with the importance of the claim and the potential damage that would occur if the claim is incorrect. For instance, a teacher might ask 3 students whether her slides are readable from the back of the classroom. A team of researchers has studied 36 firms to determine what business practices make firms successful. Data from thousands of people would be necessary before politicians could claim that there must be a major change in laws governing health care.

When the evidence is not sufficient to support a claim, we say that the author is guilty of the *fallacy of hasty generalization.* A *fallacy* is defined as an "erroneous but frequently persuasive way of being led from a reason or circumstance to a conclusion." If we jump to a conclusion based on insufficient evidence, we are engaging in fallacious thinking.

Representativeness

Let us say that an author was making a claim about the reaction of Canadians to cutbacks in government services. The author teaches at a university, so he interviews students about their attitude to cutbacks and uses these interviews as the basis for his claim. Can this be considered good evidence? No. The problem is that university students tend to be younger than Canadians in general; they also may be more educated and have less disposable income. The evidence they provide is not *representative* of all Canadians. As a rule, the variety in the sources of evidence should match the variety in the population relevant to the claim. If an author is claiming that a certain company is abusive of employees and a terrible place to work, but the only people who consented to be interviewed were people who had quit or been fired, her data may not be a fair sample. It is not representative of those employees who have continued to work happily at the firm and her claim is undermined.

The fallacy of *hasty generalization* is also relevant to unrepresentative evidence. We should not be persuaded by evidence that does not come from a fair sample of information (see Box 3-2).

Authority

Typically, we don't have first hand knowledge of the evidence when we write. Even experts have first hand knowledge of only a small sample of experience. Every one relies on the experience of others. The question is, which others? When people have special training and professional credentials, or considerable experience in a

Box 3-2: Political polls and representativeness

Can political polling predict election results? Often they can. Political polls are interesting for another reason–there is an immediate and definitive confirmation of the prediction. Polling, therefore, is one of the few areas in which researchers can determine just how representative their evidence is. If the information collected by the pollsters is drawn from an unrepresentative sample of the population, the poll results will be misleading.

A classic case occurred during the US presidential election of 1936. The editors at a news magazine called the *Literary Digest* mailed ten million postcards to voters asking them who they planned to vote for–Alf Landon or Franklin Roosevelt. Of the two million responses they received, the votes were overwhelmingly in favour of Landon. A fortnight later, Roosevelt won by the largest landslide in American history. Why had the poll been so misleading? The *Digest* developed its mailing list using telephone directories and lists of car owners. Unfortunately this created a sample with a bias in favour of the wealthy; only richer people could afford cars and telephones in those days. Poorer people were more likely to vote for Roosevelt as his political platform stressed jobs for the unemployed.

In the same election, another poll predicted the result accurately. This poll was an early success of George Gallup, who had used a more representative sample. Yet even the famous Gallup polls have proved erroneous; their poll in 1948 predicted that Thomas Dewey would win the presidential election over Harry Truman. One of the explanations for their failure was that their sampling procedure under-represented people who lived in cities and over-represented people from rural areas. Since it was largely city people who favoured Truman, the number of their votes was under-estimated by Gallup's poll.

Babbie, E. (1983). *The practice of social research, 3rd edition*, Wadsworth Publishing Co, Belmont, California.

particular area, we call them *authorities* and pay close attention to the evidence they provide. When writers cite business scholars and experienced business people, this lends authority to their arguments. The currency of the source is important. Apart from the classics in any subject, current writing is usually more authoritative than older sources, particularly in rapidly-changing fields where new discoveries are important.

In addition, authority is context-dependent. A legal argument needs, first and foremost, authoritative legal sources, while scientific writing will cite the evidence produced by other scientists. On the other hand, we should be less persuaded when a film star endorses a particular snack food or a sports hero is used to convince us of the efficiency of an airline; in both cases, the endorsers are providing evidence outside their area of expertise. This is termed the *fallacy of false appeal to authority*, which we commit when we accept the testimony of someone who has no expertise in the relevant area. Sadly, advertisers know how easy it is for us to succumb to this fallacy!

Another fallacy that is related to the source of the evidence is the fallacy of *argumentum ad populum* which, loosely translated, means "appeal to the people." The mere fact that many people accept a belief is not in itself evidence that the belief is correct. This fallacy has also been called the *bandwagon effect*. If a manager claims that getting a web-site would be good for the company just because "everybody is on the web these days," he may be falling prey to the fallacy of *argumentum ad populum*, especially if he has no independent basis for the belief apart from the knowledge that others are doing it. He is also presuming, perhaps erroneously, that other firms exercised good judgement when they decided to create company web-sites.

Clarity of expression
The significance of the evidence should be clearly stated. A common failing is that authors provide information as evidence, but they are not explicit about what this information signifies. Often it is the use of tables, figures, charts or graphs that creates this problem. In our discussion of precision above, we noted that quantitative data can be quite persuasive. It must, however, always be interpreted for the reader. Numbers do not speak for themselves. Consider the following table:

Firm	Grievance rate	Absence rate	Firm performance
1	8.2	3.97	2.7
2	3.2	3.00	6.1
3	6.5	2.71	4.6
4	7.4	2.38	3.3
5	2.6	1.84	4.9

Quite precise, but what does it mean? The author should summarize the table, explaining the meaning of the numbers and telling us clearly that he interprets the numbers as showing that unhappy employees, defined as those who file grievances and are absent relatively often, undermine the performance of the firm. Once the evidence is expressed with clarity, the table begins to take on some meaning, and we can then see how it might bolster the author's claim that good people management improves business success. So, too, should direct quotations be clearly interpreted when they are offered in evidence.

A sample analysis

Let us look again at the passage above that claims that students today are more knowledgeable than they were in the past. Here is a sample response that evaluates the quality of the evidence presented, and discusses whether, on the whole, the reader is persuaded by the argument.

> **Accuracy** I have independent information that suggests that some aspects of the data are accurate. For one thing, I have heard on TV about government initiatives to make daycare more affordable for the increasingly large number of dual-career couples and single parents, so perhaps that means that more children are indeed attending daycare compared with ten years ago. On the other hand, I have no means of judging the accuracy of the statements about what kids actually learn in daycare. Second, my uncle is a teacher and a few years ago he went back to school to do a graduate diploma so he could continue in his career. In general it is well known that teachers have increasingly been required to seek higher education in order to obtain the positions they want. However I am unable to

evaluate the accuracy of the comment that teachers are trained in teaching more frequently than they used to be ten years ago. And as far as computers go, there is no question in my mind that nowadays more people have computers and Internet connections; the falling prices and conversations with my friends and acquaintances make this obvious to me. In summary, my evaluation of accuracy is mixed. I need to find other clues before I'd be willing to accept the evidence as accurate in its entirety.

Precision The information is fairly general. The author talks about *the prevalence of daycare.* It would have been more convincing if I had been given a percentage of children in daycare now, compared with a percentage ten years ago. Also *most high school teachers* is not precise. Even the statistic that *more than 50% of Canadian families* have one or more computers at home should have been more precise. There are no specific quotes presented. To my mind, the low precision detracts from the argument. In fact, if more precise numbers had been given throughout, it might have encouraged me to believe that the author had done careful research, which would create a more positive evaluation of *accuracy* as well.

Sufficiency Three different pieces of evidence are presented. For a text of this length, this might be deemed sufficient, especially since the claim does not have important policy implications. In other words, the truth or falsity of the claim may make for lively Sunday dinner conversations, but it is unlikely to affect education policies or practices. So I am satisfied that three pieces of evidence is sufficient for this claim.

Representativeness The types of evidence are quite varied, including evidence about how people learn in early childhood as well as when they are older students. Evidence includes both the content of knowledge (the three Rs, Internet information and teachers' knowledge of their disciplines) as well as the process of gaining knowledge (teaching skills, the convenience and efficiency of the Internet). I might have expected to see some comparison of the school curricula then and now, but in general I am moderately satisfied with the diversity, or representativeness, of this evidence.

Authority I don't know who the author of this piece is, or what are his or her qualifications and expertise. Nor are any other authorities actually mentioned in the text. At one point, the author says that he or she *read in the newspaper* a particular bit of evidence, but does not even mention which newspaper it was. I might have been a respected publication like the *Globe and Mail* or it might have been a neighbourhood weekly where the contributors may be less careful of their facts. It might even have been a computer news publication which might be biassed in favour of overstating the percent of computer ownership. The absence of any controlled scientific research detracts from the authority. The opinions of an experienced teacher might also have helped, but as it stands, the text has very low authority. If there had been more authoritative information it might also have helped to convince me that the evidence is **accurate**.

Clarity of expression The text is easy to read because it is quite clearly expressed. The points are laid out in simple sentences with the claim explicitly stated at the beginning and the evidence summarized at the end.

Overall, my reaction to this argument is mixed. While the evidence appears to be sufficient, representative and clearly expressed, I remain uncertain about the accuracy, especially since the precision and authority are so weak. The author needs to do more work if s/he is to convince me that I should accept the claim based on this evidence.

Other objections

As you read the analysis above, you may have objected to yet another aspect of the argument. If you believe that children learn just as much at home with a parent or nanny as they learn in a daycare, or that however early kids are taught, by eight years of age there is no difference in knowledge, then the increasing use of daycare will not be deemed *relevant* to the claim. If you think that most of the time on the Internet is spent in chat groups, visiting salacious web-sites or sending electronic mail to friends, then you will not accept that widespread use of technology is *relevant* to increased knowledge among students. If you believe that people's greater expertise is unrelated to how well they can communicate with lay-persons, then the advanced degrees of today's teachers will not be seen as *relevant*. All these issues of relevance are related to your **underlying assumptions**, which is the topic of the next chapter.

Effective writing

When we study an issue and report our findings, we should present our argument in the form of a claim and supporting evidence. For complex arguments, each piece of evidence may be treated in turn as if it were a claim, and further, more detailed evidence is presented in explanation. Provide your readers with the wherewithal to determine whether your evidence is sound. Citing the sources of your evidence allows your readers to judge the *authority,* and so the *accuracy* of our the information. (Of course, we also cite the sources because it is essential, when we use other people's ideas, to give credit where credit is due). Your readers will judge the authority of your views as a writer, too, since the selection of inappropriate or inaccurate sources reflects on the writer's judgement. Remember that one of the purposes of writing is to join the authority chain as well, if only in the eyes of the reader. If the claim is controversial, you must recognize this and not assume that one piece of evidence is *sufficient.* As well, note that when more than one authority must be cited, and the selection must be *representative.* Even if the readers cannot themselves describe the range of serious views, they can see quickly enough if your selection of evidence has the appearance of being fair. Recall, too, that appropriate *precision* and *clear* statements of the significance of your evidence are crucial. Avoid the over-use of abstract, ambiguous words in your writing.

Resource material for additional reading:

Booth, W., Coulomb, G. & Williams, J. (1995). *The craft of research*, University of Chicago Press. The listing of the various aspects of the quality of evidence draws on the work of the authors.
Browne, N. & Keeley, S. (1994). *Asking the right questions*, Prentice Hall.
Chaffee, J. (1997). *Thinking critically*, 5th edition, Houghton Mifflin Co.

Exercise 3-1: Evaluate the evidence

Read the passage below and state the major claim that is being made. Identify and evaluate the evidence that is presented for the claim, discussing its accuracy, sufficiency, precision, representativeness, authority and clarity of expression.

Skyrocketing executive pay has contributed to the demise of morale and productivity in Canadian society. Salary rises have been dizzying. In the past a senior management compensation package of $1 million was rare, yet in 1997, at least ten executives received salary and benefits in the eight-figure range, and the typical compensation package offered to chief executive officers grew by 112 percent. The average pay of CEOs in Toronto was almost $354,000 in 1999, an increase of 55 percent since 1993. This figure does not even include stock options, the fastest-growing portion of the CEO compensation package. And in the US, the situation is even more extreme. In 1996, a $39.8 million compensation and stock option packet was offered to General Electric chief executive officer, Jack Welch. Green Tree Financial Corp's CEO Lawrence Coss received a $102.5 million bonus and was granted $38.8 million in stock options. US CEOs average twice the pay that Canadian executives receive. Diane Francis of the Financial Post believes that executive compensation is currently "one of the biggest scandals in North America."

Now consider the employees. The 1990s marked a decade of salary freezes, lay-offs and job obsolescence. Listen to the words of a 50-year old plant manager for an automotive company. "It looks as though I'll not get a salary adjustment this year because of the budget cuts. There's also talk of another lay-off. I can't afford to lose my job—I have a family to support with two kids in university. I just don't get it. Last year we had to let go of over 1,000 of our employees, yet our president is raking in more than five million dollars. Damn, we're upset! He's making the shareholders rich by eliminating our jobs and he gets rewarded with millions. The message is clear. They don't really care about employees. They only care about themselves and how much money they can make for themselves."

By reducing executive pay, employee morale and productivity will improve since employees will no longer feel as though they are working solely to generate the CEO's multi-million dollar bonus.

Exercise 3-2
Read the passage below and state the major claim that is being made. Identify and evaluate the evidence that is presented for the claim, discussing its accuracy, sufficiency, precision, representativeness, authority and clarity of expression.

Question: Who is best placed to evaluate managers? Answer: Anybody who has interactions with them. Tradition has it that the person who is one step above the manager in the organization's hierarchy is the prime evaluator, but it is clear that anyone who interacts with the manager on the job can provide valuable feedback about the manager's performance—this may include peers, subordinates, and even customers and suppliers.

Managers nowadays often work in teams, collaborating and coordinating their efforts with co-workers in other divisions or departments. Furthermore, today's managers supervise workers who are more educated and technically skilled than was the norm 25 years ago. These "knowledge workers," who oftentimes know more than the managers themselves about particular tasks, need to be stimulated and inspired, rather than simply told what to do.

In addition to supervising a new breed of worker, managers today operate in a business environment that is characterised by rapid and unpredictable change. They must keep interacting with suppliers, customers and other people outside the organization, all of whom can provide valuable information that will keep the firm competitive.

What can we demand of managers, then? The flexibility to adapt to changing technologies and market conditions; the ability to involve subordinates in decision making so as to employ their talents most fully; and skill at articulating an inspiring vision that energizes subordinates and stimulates them to maximal performance. The managers' peers, subordinates, suppliers and customers are in an excellent position to assess these characteristics in an accurate and fair manner. The system of performance evaluation that elicits feedback from this variety of sources is called 360 degree feedback; this system has been deemed one of the most important recent advances in human resources by management scholars, consultants, and business executives alike. Companies like Petro-Canada, Coca-Cola, DuPont and Disney Corporation have all used variants of the 360 degree technique.

Self-evaluation is also part of 360 degree assessment. If the manager can say, for example: "I feel that my skills at generating new business are weak, and my peers and subordinates agree with me," this is the first step in the development process. Having such issues emerge in a self-evaluation also puts the responsibility on the boss to provide training or support for the managers. It has been the experience of many companies that even if the ultimate responsibility for performance evaluation stays with the boss, 360 degree evaluation has an appreciable positive impact on managers' skills, motivation and performance.

Exercise 3-3: Evaluate the evidence. *Read the passage below and state the major claim that is being made. Identify and evaluate the evidence that is presented for the claim, discussing its accuracy, sufficiency, precision, representativeness, authority and clarity of expression.*

That Tommy Hilfiger sweatshirt you are wearing, is it genuine? Why are those Rolex watches at the flea market are so cheap? Why does that CD have a photocopied label instead of a real printed one? A sea of counterfeit merchandise surrounds us. Industry analysts estimate that pirated music recordings reached as high as 1.5 billion audiotapes and 350 million CDs in 1996. About five percent of all watches sold, 5% of perfumes and 12% of toys carry counterfeit labels. In Canada, data collected by Pricewaterhouse-Coopers suggest that unauthorized copies comprise 39% of all computer software.

These and other estimates are described in an investigative report by David Lees, a journalist writing for the *Financial Post Magazine*. Counterfeiting is a mammoth problem and one that is very difficult to control, primarily, writes Lees, because of "a lack of political will." Lees deplores the attitude of people, politicians included, who seem to feel that counterfeiting is only a minor crime. If a car is stolen, the owner no longer has his property, but if a brand name is copied, so what? The rich, faceless corporation that owns the brand still has its merchandise! Such are the attitudes that make counterfeiting seem like a victimless crime. But, he argues, our casual attitude to counterfeiting is a mistake. At the worst, some fakes are life-threatening; notably, fake pharmaceuticals have caused deaths in the Third World and counterfeit air plane replacement parts have led to fatal plane crashes.

Of course there are laws in place which prohibit counterfeiting–violators can be fined up to one million dollars and be imprisoned for up to five years. But the law is very poorly enforced. Lees reports that only one person has ever gone to jail for breaking the counterfeit law, and then only for 60 days. Canada Customs does not stop fake merchandise at the border, claiming that it has neither the expertise nor the authority to decide whether goods are genuine or fake. Instead of just going through the motions, the Canadian government must act decisively to stem this flood of counterfeit merchandise.

Exercise 3-4: Evaluate the evidence in the recent business news

Using this week's business newspapers, find an article that proposes a **contestable claim**. State the claim in one or two sentences, paraphrasing it if necessary for clarity. What evidence is presented for the claim? Evaluate the evidence in terms of *accuracy, sufficiency, precision, representativeness, authority* and *clarity of expression.*

Exercise 3-5: Collecting evidence

Here is a list of claims. In your opinion, are they more likely to be true or false? If you had to collect evidence from various sources to support or refute these claims, where would you look? Think of the qualities of good evidence to ensure that you have the information to build the best possible case for your viewpoint. For each claim, provide a list of potential sources of evidence.

Choose one of the claims and follow up on the sources of evidence that you listed. Evaluate the evidence you find in terms of its *precision, sufficiency, representativeness* and *authority.*

1. Over recent years there has been a rapid increase in e-commerce, that is, doing business on the Internet.

2. The price of university textbooks outstrips their usefulness.

3.   Having a pet does wonders for one's physical and psychological health, particularly for elderly people who live alone.

4.   Women's management styles are different from men's.

5.   The arrival of skilled immigrants in Quebec more than makes up for the so-called "brain-drain" to the United States and Ontario.

Source material for exercises:

Barnett, V. (1999). Judged by your peers, *Montreal Gazette*, 29 March.
Lees, D. (1998). Knocking off the knockoffs, *Financial Post Magazine*, December, p. 58ff.

4 Underlying assumptions

Mammon Corporation spent over two million dollars on management consultants during the years 1995-97. Much of the money was spent on business process re-engineering; several business units were eliminated and hundreds of employees lost their jobs through downsizing. A journalist writing about Mammon's recent performance claims that the money spent on these consulting engagements was wasted. Why? In reviewing the firm's last annual report, she notes that profits reported in 1998 were no higher than they were throughout the mid-nineties.

If we translate this case into our critical thinking terms, we can state it this way:
Claim: Mammon Corporation wasted money on re-engineering consultants.
Evidence: Over two million dollars was spent, but profitability has stayed about the same.

Are we persuaded by her claim that the money was wasted? Only if we agree that the 1998 profitability figures are *relevant* to the claim. In other words, do we agree that the 1998 profits *should count as evidence* that money was wasted? The general principle that connects the claim to the evidence is that "If money is spent to improve a business, but profits do not go up the next year, the money has been wasted." This principle is an *underlying assumption*. It is a logical link that fills the gap between the evidence and the claim.

Some readers may decide that the journalist's underlying assumption is sound. Re-engineering is a painful and costly process, and if the pay-off for the firm is minimal, then indeed the money was wasted. Other readers may question the assumption. Perhaps there *was* a significant improvement in performance, but economic conditions in the industry were much worse in 1998. If Mammon had not engaged in re-engineering, it might be in receivership today. Keeping profits from falling is excellent performance under such conditions! Perhaps the money spent on financial packages for departing employees reduced profits this year, but since this was a one-time extraordinary charge, we might expect that future profits will be much higher if the re-engineering decision were correct.

As critical thinkers, we must find and state the author's underlying assumptions. What are the suppositions upon which the argument is based? What must we believe if we are to see the evidence as relevant to the claim being made? Subjecting underlying assumptions to careful scrutiny is an important step in the critique of a text. Even when the evidence is of good quality–accurate, precise, clearly expressed, authoritative, sufficient and representative, the argument is not acceptable if the underlying assumptions are questionable.

Why are they "underlying?"
We said earlier that underlying assumptions are usually found in the gap that separates claims and evidence. But why does this gap exist? Shouldn't authors be more careful to show exactly why every piece of evidence is relevant to the claim? Why are underlying assumptions generally *implicit* instead of *explicit*? In other words, why are assumptions "underlying?" The answer is that once a person's assumptions about a certain topic are formed, they are the foundation of everything she thinks, says and does on that topic. They are deeply ingrained and taken for granted. It is quite rare that she would think consciously about the assumption. It simply becomes part of her tacit belief system–as natural as walking and breathing. This taken-for-grantedness of our assumptions is true for all of us.

For example, a common assumption in our society is that children should learn how to read and write. Basic education is valued. Even when we complain about the school system, we do not wonder whether or not literacy is a good thing–its value is taken for granted. This assumption is the foundation of many debates about child labour. An activist might claim that consumers should boycott factory goods like carpets and shoes that come from the labour of children in certain Third World countries. Evidence: Children work long hours in these factories, and have neither the time nor the freedom to go to school–they remain illiterate. The activist does not usually add: "And being literate is a good thing." This underlying assumption is taken for granted by both the activist and his readers or listeners.

So there is nothing wrong, really, with having unstated underlying assumptions. Authors who leave them out are not necessarily hiding them or trying to fool us. They are just taking them for granted as we all do. The only problem is that different people have different assumptions, reflecting different values. Other assumptions represent matters of fact–beliefs about reality–and they may be quite wrong or, at least, debatable. (We will return to value and reality assumptions in a later section). So uncovering assumptions and making them explicit is an important step in evaluating any argument. The process allows us to judge whether the evidence is relevant or appropriate support for the claim, and so, whether we should accept the claim. Needless to say, we tend to pay most attention to an author's underlying assumptions when they conflict with our own point of view! It is an important discipline, however, to examine assumptions explicitly even when we agree with the author's claim.

How to find underlying assumptions

In essence, one finds underlying assumptions by looking at what people write, then making guesses about what they must believe to have written that. One looks for the gap between the evidence and the claim by asking: *What must be true if the claim is to follow from this evidence? What general principle might link this particular claim to this particular evidence?* Sometimes it is useful to put oneself in the role of the writer. *What beliefs might I expect from this type of person?* For example, if you were role-playing a CEO (downsized worker, consultant, shareholder), what would you think about the evidence about consultants being a waste of money for Mammon Corporation? Other times, it is useful to be a devil's advocate: *Could someone believe this evidence and still disagree with the claim? Why?*

Sometimes finding underlying assumptions is easy because the gap between evidence and claim is a small one. Sometimes, however, the gap is large and pinning down the assumptions is quite difficult. When an author is very knowledgeable about a complex topic, she may leave large gaps in her logical connections between claims and evidence. She may be taking it for granted that her readers are also very familiar with the topic. Furthermore, when a person feels strongly about a claim, his emotions may overtake the logical presentation of his ideas and reasoning, and large gaps between evidence and claim may result.

Consider the following example: Recently I was listening to a radio talk show that was dealing with the topic of the North American Free Trade Agreement, trying to assess the aggregate benefits and costs to Canadians since NAFTA was signed in 1989. One participant maintained that free trade had proved to be a very bad idea. He described an experience that, in his view, demonstrated conclusively the problems of free trade. Here's the evidence he presented (summarized and paraphrased):

> *My favourite shoes have always been Clark's Wallabies. You know Clark's–the British shoe company. I've worn those shoes all my life; they are so comfortable. Some years ago, however, they disappeared from the shelves. I couldn't find them anywhere. Finally, a shoe store offered to order them specially for me. But when the shoes arrived, I could see right away that something was wrong. The soles were an odd, pale colour and they looked really awful. They didn't fit properly, and to add insult to injury, they cost more than I had ever paid for a pair of Wallabies in the past. I looked inside under the tongue to check the size. The size was correct, but it also said: Made in China! There, in a nutshell, is the problem with free trade!*

Briefly put, we have:

> Claim: Free trade is a bad idea
> Evidence: The Chinese-made shoes had the wrong colour, the wrong fit and were very expensive.

What, one may justifiably ask, does this disappointing shoe order have to do with free trade? Why is this evidence relevant to his claim? From his tone, it seemed so clear to him that this evidence was telling! If it is not so obvious to you, you are not alone. It requires some thought to make his underlying assumptions explicit. Here is an interpretation of what he *might* have said had he been pressed to explain the link between the evidence and his claim:

1. Free trade has opened the floodgates to products made in less developed countries.
2. Because labour is cheap in less developed countries like China, the cost of manufacturing products there is low.
3. The quality of these products is also very low, for example, many shoes made in the less developed countries are of poor quality.
4. People in Canada are sensitive to price and like the opportunity to buy cheap

shoes.

5.   Traditional, high-quality shoe manufacturers cannot compete at these prices. They either go out of business or start making their shoes in the less developed countries as well, in which case the shoes are lower in quality.

Therefore the argument: My new Wallabies are low-quality because of free trade.

Assumptions #1, 2, 4 & 5 seem necessary to explain why Wallabies are now made in China. Most economists would agree that these assumptions are reasonable. Assumption #3 seems necessary to explain why he does not like the quality of his new Wallabies. Note that complex arguments often conceal *multiple* underlying assumptions.

The next stage for the critical thinker is evaluating these underlying assumptions. Is #3 an accurate assumption? This is debatable. His could just be a subjective preference, and other people might find the new shoes look and fit just fine. Moreover, #1, 2, 4 & 5 seem inconsistent with his statement that the shoes are expensive. How could the shoes from less developed countries have undermined the market for high quality shoes if they were not cheaper? In his price comparison, has he taken inflation into account? Is he taking into account the fact that perhaps he is being charged more for this special order? In sum, we will need some more careful explanations before we accept the story of the shoes as relevant evidence for the undesirability of free trade.

Reconstructing and evaluating underlying assumptions sometimes requires that we *learn more* about issues and a variety of points of view. Knowledge of economics helps us to flesh out the assumptions being made about free trade. As you continue to take courses in business, your knowledge base will increase, which will allow you to detect underlying assumptions more easily, and to be able to judge their worth.

Reality assumptions

There are two major types of assumptions, *reality assumptions* and *value assumptions*. Reality assumptions are our beliefs about what events have taken place, what exists or how things work in the world. In other words, they are our beliefs about reality, the way things really are. Our first-hand experiences, our conversations with others, the things we read or see on television–all these shape our beliefs. In particular, when we have considerable experience that is consistent with a given belief, the belief becomes *taken for granted*. The example given in the section above is based on reality assumptions about the economics of free trade. We can guess that the man on the radio talk show had developed these ideas about how international trade works through reading, conversation, and his experiences as a consumer over many years.

Another reality assumption was encountered in the previous chapter in the text that claimed that students are more knowledgeable now than they used to be. One piece of evidence offered was that teachers have more advanced degrees nowadays than was the case in the past. The evidence is relevant only on condition that: a) People with advanced degrees have more and better quality knowledge; and b) they can pass this better knowledge-base on to students effectively. These two underlying assumptions describe the author's taken-for-granted beliefs about what makes a teacher effective. Box 4-1 presents another example of reality assumptions in organizations.

Box 4-1: Reality assumptions about employees

It's human nature for people to do as little work as they can get away with; the average employee is indolent, unambitious and dislikes responsibility. Employees must be supervised closely or they will not work to fulfill organizational goals. If, however, they are given enough money, they will generally accept direction and will be productive.

These assumptions about employees are the basis of the motivational policies, practices and programs of many firms. Douglas McGregor, a management scholar, coined the term **Theory X** to label this set of beliefs. McGregor proposed that Theory X assumptions were an inadequate description of human motivation. He made an alternative set of propositions which he called **Theory Y:** *People are not passive or lazy by nature. They only become so because that is how they are treated in organizations. The capacity for assuming responsibility and using creativity and imagination to further organizational goals does exist in employees. It is up to managers to create the organizational conditions that will release employees' potential.*

McGregor first formulated Theory X and Theory Y over forty years ago. In those days, Theory X, with its focus on external control of behaviour, was the conventional view. McGregor described Theory Y, which relied on self-control and self-direction, as a bold and innovative proposal.

Challenging reality assumptions

Once an author's reality assumptions are made explicit, the next step is to evaluate their accuracy. As mentioned above, this usually consists of critiquing the quality of the assumptions. In the free trade example, we could argue that the assumptions were logically inconsistent, and did not take into account important economic variables such as inflation. Another way of challenging reality assumptions is to provide data that would show that the assumption is incorrect. In the "knowledgeable students" example, we might show that people who have developed great expertise often find it *harder* to communicate their knowledge to lay people since they have forgotten what it was like to be so naive. We might present data to show that only a small percentage of graduate programs offer serious training in how to teach. *In general, to challenge reality assumptions we must present information showing that the author's notions of reality and how the world works are debatable or just plain wrong.*

Arguably, management today is still dominated by Theory X reality assumptions. For example, when managers install systems to monitor employees' use of the Internet during working hours, they are acting on Theory X assumptions. They may believe that without control employees will spend company time in frivolous surfing of the net. Firms that hire roving, "mystery" customers to check up on the service provided by their sales representatives are reflecting a Theory X assumption that without this surveillance, employees would be lackadaisical or rude. It is true that we do hear a lot about empowerment and self-managing teams nowadays. These are practices that are consistent with a Theory Y framework. But we have to ask ourselves whether these terms represent a true change in management assumptions—one often has the impression that managers are just paying lip service to these ideas; all the while their actual behaviour is thoroughly "X."

McGregor anticipated that progress toward the goal of Theory Y would be slow and difficult. After generations of Theory X management, it was unlikely that employees or managers could shift to a Theory Y framework overnight. Clearly many firms are taking steps in the direction of Theory Y, but it is equally clear that Theory X continues to be the predominant reality assumption among managers today.

McGregor, D. (1957). The human side of enterprise, *Management Review*, November, 41-49.

Value assumptions

Values are our ideals, our standards of right and wrong, the way things ought to be. We can recognize them through the use of words like *ought, should, desirable, unacceptable*, and so on: "You should keep your promises;"

"Teachers ought to treat students fairly;" "Cooperative work is desirable." Often, values are learned early in childhood from our parents, teachers, classmates, or through religion; other values are adopted later on, in our adult lives. Some values are very commonly held: being honest, helping those less fortunate than ourselves, having the freedom to express our views as citizens are widely seen as good things. In the world of business there are many specific values that embody our ideas of what is right and wrong. Bosses *ought* to be helpful and encouraging to their subordinates. They *ought not* to use their power to gain sexual favours. Large, successful companies

---

Box 4-2: Competitiveness as a value

"Life has become for us an endless succession of contests." Thus begins a critique by author Alfie Kohn of the value our society places on competitiveness. Throughout our school years, he notes, we are trained to compete, to think of our classmates as standing in the way of our own success. The entire economic system is based on competition: "It is not enough that we struggle against our colleagues at work to be more productive; we also must compete for the title of Friendliest Employee." Even when we socialize with people from other departments of the organization or other companies, this often takes the form of competitive games like softball or golf.

The examples of competitiveness in the world of business are countless. Margaret Wente, a journalist with the *Globe and Mail* newspaper, notes that "the prevailing metaphors of business are borrowed from the battlefield. Your competition is the enemy, and your job is to grind them to dust. Takeovers are battles. Marketing is warfare." The legendary Ray Kroc, the founder of McDonald's restaurant chain, once said: "What do you do when your competitor is drowning? Get a live hose and stick it in his throat!" Ricardo Petrella works in forecasting in the European Community Commission and decries what he calls the "gospel of competitiveness." One negative outcome he describes is accelerating obsolescence—firms must constantly develop new products, not because

---

should exhibit social responsibility by making donations to community, cultural or sporting events, and by not polluting the environment. Businesses *should* adopt strategies that allow them to stay competitive (see Box 4-2)

Although there is widespread agreement about some values in our society, *value conflicts* are also quite common. Because I value honesty, I might feel I should tell the boss about my co-worker who confessed to me that he'd lied about his qualifications for the job. You might disagree, feeling that I shouldn't tell the boss since you value loyalty to one's peer group. Sometimes these value conflicts happen within the individual. When approached by a beggar, one may feel torn between compassion and the feeling that people ought to work for their living. Values may be *ranked* differently by different people. Some people feel much more strongly about corporate social responsibility or sexual harassment, for example, than others do.

---

there is anything wrong with the old ones, but just because of the pressure to stay ahead of the competition.

Even when individuals or groups are not directly competing with one another, we seem to have an urge to compile rankings of who is best and who is not. Business magazines regularly publish lists of the top 100 firms, cutting across diverse industries. News magazines report on the best universities in the country. In the summer of 1999, a ranking of the wealthiest Canadians was made public. Ken Thompson, chairman of the publishing company, Thompson Corp, with a net worth of just under $21 billion, was in the number one position. One is tempted to wonder: What exactly is the point of this ranking? Earlier in the same year, there was great concern because of a report by a Washington DC think tank which claimed that Canada's ranking in ability to innovate slipped from #6 to #9 over a ten-year period. What does that mean to us? To others?

For many people, competitiveness is seen not just as the best way of doing things, but as "a fact of life" that is, the *only* way of doing things. Are there viable alternatives? One such alternative is cooperation–working with others, says Alfie Kohn. Or independence–comparing oneself not to others, but to an objective or self-set standard.

Kohn, A. (1992). *No Contest*, Revised edition, Houghton Mifflin.
Lamey, M. (1992). Downside seen to competitiveness, *Montreal Gazette*, 8 June.
Wente, M. (1997). Why I'll never be CEO, *Globe and Mail*, 25 October, D7.

Challenging value assumptions

Value conflicts and differential value rankings are reasons for disagreements about the relevance of the evidence presented for a claim. In the following example, three business students are discussing the team paper about a successful company which they must write for one of their courses.

> **Rosa**: We should do our paper on Hotshot Inc. It's a great company.
>
> **Katy**: Why do you think Hotshot is so great?
>
> **Rosa**: Its founder is fabulously wealthy, he's worth billions! And it's all from this one company.
>
> **Tom**: Yes, she's right. I've read a lot about Mr. Hotshot and his company in the newspapers, and the company's share prices have been climbing steadily for years now.
>
> **Katy**: Well I don't think that Hotshot's so wonderful. Sure, the top guys are making a lot of money, but the company is horribly exploitative. They treat their employees like dog turds, and they use strong-arm techniques to squeeze out their smaller competitors.
>
> **Rosa**: But that's just business. You can't argue with success!

Rosa and Tom clearly value the *material success* of the entrepreneur and owners, whereas Katy places more importance on *corporate social responsibility* as a measure of what makes a firm successful. Katy does not deny the accuracy of the evidence provided about Mr. Hotshot's financial worth and the return on shareholders' investments. She just does not believe that profits are the most important aspect of what makes a great firm, so the financial information is dismissed as irrelevant. Rosa and Tom, with their focus on monetary worth may also accept the characterization of Hotshot's business strategies, but they maintain that these practices are of little importance in evaluating the company. Each side could continue to add more evidence about financial success or about business strategies, but the additional evidence would not persuade the other side since the disagreement about the underlying value assumptions remains. Can Katy persuade the other two that Hotshot's billions are not worthy of consideration? Can Rosa and Tom convince Katy that Hotshot's aggressive tactics are perfectly acceptable? It might be difficult in either case.

Values, as we have said, are often developed early in life and are quite resistant to change. It is not easy to make a profiteer out of someone who has been taught early in life that the love of money is the root of all evil. In the same way, it might take an extraordinary and jolting personal experience to create an iconoclast out of someone who has always believed in the value of obedience to authority. Not all values are so deep-seated, of course, but our value preferences form a significant part of our self-concept and are not relinquished lightly. In general, challenging value assumptions is a more difficult task than challenging descriptive assumptions. *The task of the critical thinker becomes one of demonstrating that the author's argument is rooted in a particular, idiosyncratic set of value assumptions. Since other people might have a different but equally valid set of values, the argument is therefore not universally acceptable.*

Effective writing

Critical thinking about underlying assumptions can help you to improve your own writing. A large quantity of evidence for your claims, and ensuring that the evidence is of good quality are both necessary but not enough to be convincing. It is also important to make it clear that each piece of evidence is relevant. As you compose your text, articulate all your underlying assumptions and examine them with care. Keep asking yourself questions like: *Is this assumption always true? Are there circumstances in which the reality assumptions might not hold? Are there people whose value preferences might be different or in conflict with your own? Are all of the assumptions that underlie your argument logically consistent with one another?* This self-questioning will allow you to understand the foundations of your own reasoning, and to spot any weaknesses in your argument before your readers do. One method that aids self-questioning about conflicting assumptions is the development of **invented dialogues**, described in Box 4-3.

Next you must decide which of the assumptions you should include explicitly in the text and which can be left unstated. You may find that the majority of the assumptions are so obvious that they may remain implicit. But take care! What seems obvious to you may not be obvious to all your readers. In particular, if you can think of any circumstances in which your reality assumptions might not be true, it is best to describe these scenarios explicitly and limit your argument accordingly. Think about who your audience is likely to be. If they do not share your values, your carefully-compiled evidence will be seen as irrelevant or wrong-headed. Think about the type of evidence that would be convincing for your expected readers. State your value preferences explicitly and argue for them so that your audience can at least appreciate your viewpoint. In the final chapter of this handbook, we will discuss *techniques of persuasion*, developing the notion of how a focus on your audience can help you to make your writing more convincing, even when your audience initially disagrees with you.

Box 4-3: Invented dialogues

A fruitful way of exploring underlying assumptions is by constructing an **invented dialogue**. You start by imagining a discussion between two people who hold reality or value assumptions that conflict. This exercise is easiest if you can think of people you actually know who have opposing views. Write a brief dialogue, about five or six exchanges from each of the two participants. Try to make their comments persuasive, lively, and natural. It often helps to read your dialogue out loud.

Here is an example of an invented dialogue between a Human Resource manager [HR] and a Vice-President, Operations [VP].

HR: Well, we've boiled it down to two potential candidates for the position. Both candidates have the relevant work experience and education. They both have impeccable track records with rave reviews from previous employers.

VP: Great! I'm looking forward to interviewing them myself.

HR: The first candidate is a woman in her mid-thirties who's been working...

VP: Hold on, a woman?!? You know we've never had a woman in this position before. She would have to supervise over 50 men. I sure hope your other candidate is a man.

HR: Come on, Eric. You know we cannot discriminate against anyone based solely on gender.

VP: Who's talking about discrimination? We're talking about a person

---

Exercise 4-1

*What is the link between the claim and the evidence presented in the statements below? Describe the general principle that is the **underlying assumption** in each case.*

1. I don't want to work on a team with Philip. He talks constantly and nobody can get a word in edgewise.
   Underlying assumption: People on a team should be allowed an equal contribution of ideas.

2. Gloria bought a new washing machine from Anvil Appliances last week, but it is malfunctioning. The people at Anvil should fix it or replace the machine with another.

claim: if purchase item should be under warrenty.
∴ the machine is not working.

who will fit the shop-floor culture. I'm not against hiring a woman for a middle management position, but we're talking here about the guys on the floor! They've never had to report to a woman before. Her life will be hell!

HR: Well things will have to change around here unless you prefer to have the Human Rights Commission knocking on our door. And then there's the Employment Equity Bill which says....

VP: What the devil does the government know about our shop floor? We at headquarters understand about cultural diversity, and how it makes good business sense in a global environment. But this is a particular case. We simply can't hire a woman to handle those boys in the shop. It's a pretty rough environment down there.

HR: Well with your attitude, of course it will never work. If corporate backs a woman, you'll send a clear message to everyone that we value people for their skills, not their sex or race.

VP: I can picture the guys' reaction already. I know it won't fly.

How would you characterise the conflicting assumptions of these speakers? Consider their reality and value assumptions about (a) the relative importance of education and experience; (b) compatibility with the company culture; (c) vigilance of government agencies; (d) gender roles; (e) impact of top management attitudes on workers; and so on.

Inventing dialogues of this sort can help you to clarify your own assumptions; and you train yourself to develop a richer understanding of alternative points of view.

3. Mrs. Carpenter ought to take better care of her husband. The shirt he is wearing today is not very clean and his tie doesn't match at all.

4. Traffic jams in this city are becoming intolerable. Businesses should offer flexible starting and quitting times to their employees.

claims - road infrastructures are bad; driver education system is bad

5. Angela owns a thriving hardware store, but is currently short-staffed. Since her son is unemployed, Angela should offer him a job in the store.

everyone going & leaving work @ same time

6. Mr Allard's rental rate for his vacation house is preposterously high—it's almost twice as much as he charged last year. He is taking advantage of the new golf course that has been built in the area.

claim - this person rents houses and is upset that rent ↑.

claim - families should stick together in time of need.
- son would be a good employer.

7.   That restaurant must serve good Chinese food. Look, almost everyone eating in there
is Chinese.

Exercise 4-2: Underlying assumptions and values

*Identify the claim and evidence in each paragraph. Discuss the underlying assumptions
and values that are implicit here. In other words, what general principles link these claims
with the evidence? Do you agree with these assumptions, that is, do you believe that the
evidence relevant?*

1.   Commercial advertising should be allowed in university corridors and classrooms. In
past years, senior university administrators have been calling for more university-
business linkages; funds are sorely needed. We must expect that corporations will
want to benefit from these arrangements by promoting their products. Second,
everyone is bombarded with commercial advertisements on streets, in buses and
metros, everywhere. What difference does it make if the ads are seen after people step
into the university building? In any case, interviews show that most students and staff
hardly notice the ads in our buildings.

2.   Using the Internet causes people to become depressed and isolated. A research study
conducted with a group of family members found that there were negative
psychological effects after the family got access to the Internet. Although they did
socialize on the Internet using electronic mail, the participants were found to spend
less time with their family and friends. Most home computers are set up in a den or
bedroom, rather than a living room where the computer user is likely to be around other
people.

3.   Job-hopping, the practice of switching jobs frequently, is on the rise. One factor
contributing to this increase is the use of the Internet to post job opportunities and on-
line resumes. A study conducted in 1999 found over 500 career sites on the Web.
Nearly 45% of Canadian adults under 30 years of age have included the Internet in their
job searches. Companies today can sift through vast numbers of resumes; job seekers
now have ready access to a host of new career opportunities. Some HR managers warn
that this seeming advance in corporate recruitment is a mixed blessing. The presence of
Internet career sites mean that companies end up investing in people who only stay at
their job from 4-6 months. And the problem will only get worse in the years to come.

4.   Consumers should boycott factory goods that come from the labour of children in
certain Third World countries. Evidence shows that children work long hours in
factories producing carpets or athletic shoes, for example. They have neither the time
nor the freedom to go to school–they remain illiterate. There are also statistics that
show the high incidence of stunted growth of children in countries that allow child

[handwritten margin notes:]
Internet is facilitating ppl in finding diff jobs.
- giving them more options. vice versa
- ppl who look for jobs on the internet won't be good employees
- employees are less reliable

labour. Finally, these countries often have the highest unemployment rates among adults.

5. People continue to smoke against the advice of their doctors, therefore they should be put on the bottom of hospital waiting lists. There have been reports of British doctors who give lower priority to coronary operations for patients who persist in smoking. This would make good sense for the over-extended Canadian health system.

6. The US Consumer Product Safety Association has concluded that adult beds are dangerous products as far as babies are concerned. A 1999 research study reviewed death certificates over a seven-year period and estimated that 64 infant deaths occur each year when babies sleep with their parents. The Association recommends that the practice of parents sleeping with their infants be outlawed. Many parents have reacted to this study with anger, noting that babies have slept with their parents since time immemorial, and the practice provides the attention, security and nurturing that are essential for happy, healthy family life.

Exercise 4-3: Advertising and underlying assumptions

A rich source of practice in uncovering and evaluating underlying assumptions is in the area of commercial advertising. Read the information in the box below, then do the exercise which follows.

> Some advertisements provide clear evidence for their claim that you should buy the manufacturer's product. They give you *relevant* information showing how use of the product will fulfil your needs, satisfy your desires or solve your problems. Thus, for example, if you learn from an ad that a particular line of baked goods is made from whole grains with low sugar content, and you have been trying to make improvements in your diet and health, then the evidence in the ad is relevant to the claims that you should use these baked goods.
>
> But you will also see some ads that do not provide relevant evidence. Perhaps, for example, the baked-goods advertisement just shows a scene of a smiling, grandmotherly lady in a cosy, old-fashioned kitchen, bearing a tray of cookies. Maybe it portrays an elegant table set for afternoon tea–with polished silver tea service, fine linen napkins, and the manufacturer's product. Maybe we see a well-known athlete or actor enjoying the product. Advertisements like these rely on creating feelings of pleasure or admiration within us, and associating these feelings with the product. It is an emotional appeal, and the advertisers are counting on us *not* to analyse it rationally. When we do analyse it, however, we see that the underlying assumption is "because this ad makes you feel good, you should buy our product." No direct, relevant evidence is provided, so this type of advertisement does not justify a purchase. Unfortunately these ads continue to be very successful for advertisers since so few of us think critically about the underlying assumptions.

A.   Watch television for a few hours, read a variety of popular magazines, or take a walk about town, paying special attention to the commercials, print ads or billboards that you encounter.

B.   Select three ads that provide relevant evidence about why one should purchase a product or service.

C.   Select three ads that are based on questionable underlying assumptions since they provide no relevant evidence.

D.   In each case, describe the advertisement and explain what the advertiser is doing to increase the attractiveness of the product or service.

Exercise 4-4

Review Boxes 4-1 and 4-3. Write an invented dialogue between two university professors who have Theory X and Theory Y assumptions about their undergraduate students. Alternatively, invent a dialogue on a subject of your choice.

5 Causal claims

Many of the claims authors make can be classified as causal claims. They argue that certain events or factors *(causes)* are responsible for bringing about other events or situations *(effects)*. Cause and effect relationships are an essential aspect of understanding the business environment. In fact, most of our attempts to make sense of the world around us–whenever we pose the question: *Why?*–lead to cause and effect explanations. "Why are sales of our firm's bottled soft drinks falling?" "Why are there so few women CEOs in large companies?" "Why is there currently a boom in the home renovation industry?" "Why is Professor Merton so well liked by his students?" When we provide answers for these questions, we are identifying causes for observed outcomes. For example, we may determine that soft-drink sales are falling because consumers are increasingly concerned about high sugar content in their foods. Concern for sugar content would be the cause; falling sales would be the effect in this case.

Sometimes, we know the "cause" and we are trying to predict the "effect." "What will happen if we decrease our printing budget by 15%?" "If we allow commercial advertising on the walls of public institutions like hospitals and schools, what reactions can we anticipate?" "What would be the result of allowing a merger between two large Canadian banks?" In 1998, when there was much discussion about proposed mergers between the Bank of Montreal and the Royal Bank of Canada, and the Canadian Imperial Bank of Commerce and the Toronto Dominion Bank, many consumers believed that bank mergers (cause) would lead to a decrease in bank services and an increase in their prices (effects).

Causal reasoning is natural–and useful

Trying to identify connections between causes and effects is basically human nature– as natural as breathing. Very young children start asking *Why?* as they take the first steps towards developing their understanding of the world. Much of our thinking is devoted to figuring out why things occurred and predicting what is likely to happen next. Without causal links between situations, nothing would make sense. Every event would be random and disconnected. Life would simply be a "buzzing, blooming confusion." The identification of causal relationships gives meaning to the world that surrounds us.

Cause-and-effect relationships are also the basis for decision making and reasoned action. For example, the belief that consumers' concerns about nutrition are changing might lead the marketing department of our firm to develop new products such as sugar-free, low calorie bottled soft drinks. It is also likely to change the way these products are advertised.

Causal reasoning can be very difficult

Although we recognise the importance of establishing causal relationships, it is also true that it is very difficult to do. In the complex situations we encounter in the world of business, it is sometimes difficult to find reasonable and likely causes for certain outcomes. "Why is innovativeness lower in some countries than in others?" "Why are incidents of 'road rage' on the increase in our cities?" Causes can be elusive.

Even more frequently, the difficulty in determining cause and effect links arises from the fact that outcomes may have multiple causes. Let's say you notice that winter is over and you've managed to escape your usual winter cold. Well, you think, it must be because you've been drinking that special echinacea herb tea your Aunt Minnie gave you, saying it is good for avoiding colds. You decide to call her and tell her it worked. But upon further thought, you realize there may have been other causes for your health during the season. It was an unusually mild winter with few dramatic swings of temperature. Also, since your new apartment is not far from downtown, you've been able to walk to school and your job instead of taking the bus, and so you have had less contact with other people. You've started exercising twice a week as well, and you recall reading somewhere that being in good physical shape helps to ward off colds. In short, there could have been many potential causes, so you are not sure any more that Aunt Minnie's herb tea was really a cause of your cold-free winter. The other factors on their own could well have caused your good health, quite independently of whether or not you drank the tea.

As critical thinkers, we must examine carefully the causal claims of authors. Are they describing genuine cause-effect relationships? Can we think of plausible *rival causal explanations* that would account for exactly the same events? If we can, then we do not really know whether it is the factor proposed by the author, the rival cause we came up with, or a combination of both causes that led to the observed effect. The author's claim becomes less convincing.

Let us now look at some examples of plausible rival causes. There are three types of rival causes that will concern us here: rival causes related to differences between groups; correlation between characteristics; and the *post hoc ergo propter hoc* fallacy. We will explain each of these in turn.

Differences between groups

An alumni survey produces evidence showing that graduates of Academy University are more successful on the job market than graduates of Ivory Tower University. The administrators at Academy claim that this success is caused by its superior programs–the up-to-date curriculum content, the talented teaching and the advanced technological resources available at their institution. The top-notch facilities and programs cause its students to develop excellent, marketable skills which impress company recruiters and lead to rapid and remunerative job offers. If you come to Academy University, their brochures claim, you'll do better than going to that other school.

Perhaps. But is the content of the academic programs the only difference between Academy and Ivory Tower graduates? It may turn out that Academy has more rigorous admission requirements, so the students who *enter* their programs are smarter than the Ivory Tower students to start with. Even if Academy teachers had been ditchwater-dull and used blackboard chalk instead of Powerpoint, their smart students still would have excelled on the job market. Academy is claiming that their *programs* are the cause of their comparative success. Our rival cause is that their *selectivity in admissions* causes success. It is also possible that a combination of both factors is the true (multiple) cause. Another possibility is that Academy University is in an urban centre where many students have good part-time jobs, while Ivory Tower is in a rural setting and few students have part-time jobs of any consequence. It might be, then, that it is the *work experience* of the graduates that is causing the differences in success, and the academic programs are completely irrelevant.

In general, whenever an author says that an outcome is caused by a specific difference between groups, we must pause and think: *Are there any other differences between these groups that may be relevant?* If we can think of some other relevant factor that differs between the groups, we have a plausible rival cause.

Here's another example for you to think about. It has been noted that women who choose to have their babies at home have healthier babies than women whose babies are born in the hospital. One causal explanation that has been offered is that a hospital is an uncaring, unnatural environment and is no place for the natural function of bringing babies into the world. The heavy focus on medical technology in the hospital environment, and the stress this produces in pregnant women causes physical problems in newborn infants. People who believe this explanation often recommend that if a woman stays at home, and has her baby using a the services of a midwife in familiar surroundings, there are psychological and physical benefits for both mother and child. Briefly put, the argument is that the hospital setting causes health problems in infants. Can you come up with plausible rival explanations of this relationship?

Correlation between characteristics

Here is an example of the type of writing often seen in the business press: *It is important for all companies to have a strategic vision. What does your company stand for? What are your business values and mission? How do you see your future? Your firm's vision must be clearly communicated to employees at all levels of the organization. Business scholars have studied these "visionary" companies and found that they enjoy greater long-term success than other companies whose vision is less pervasive. The more careful you are to disseminate a clear vision, the better the performance of your firm. Why? Because vision inspires employees and focuses their energies. Poor visioning leaves your resources scattered and your employees unmotivated. Start developing your vision now–don't get left behind!*

The claim here is that a stronger company vision causes better performance. A weaker vision causes poorer performance. The authors have taken a *correlation* between these two factors and are claiming a *causal* link. Their explanation that a clearly-communicated vision results in motivation and focus seems reasonable.

But is this the only explanation that will fit with the observations? Is it not possible that the link works in reverse? It may be that the better the performance of the firm, the more attention is paid to it in the media. Journalists visit the company, interview its managers and write up their description of what "makes the organization tick." The news reports are widely-read, and the readers include the firm's own employees and managers who end up with greater awareness and understanding of their company, its mission and values. In this interpretation, it is the company's stellar performance that is causing the strong vision to develop. If this rival explanation turns out to be the true, working on your company's vision is a dead-end strategy. Instead of vision causing performance, performance is actually causing vision. This is an example of *reverse causation*. In general, when two factors, A and B, are correlated, it may be that A is causing B, but it is also possible that B is causing A.

Yet another interpretation must be considered. Sometimes two factors may be strongly correlated, but there is no causal link at all between the two. It is well known, for instance, that when ice-cream consumption is high in a given year, the rate of heart attacks among the population is also very high. It would be absurd to suggest that eating ice-cream brings on a heart attack within a year. It would be even more ridiculous to claim that when one has a heart attack, this creates a craving for ice-cream. Neither direct causation nor reverse causation is likely. The correlation is high because there is a *third factor* that is linked to both ice-cream consumption and heart attacks. This third factor, of course, is heat. The hotter the temperature, the more ice-cream is eaten, and the hotter it gets, the greater the number of people who succumb to heart attacks. No matter how strong the correlation between two variables, we cannot automatically assume there is a causal connection.

The ice-cream/heart-attack example is clear-cut, but in other cases it may be harder to see that causal links are not really there. Returning to the case of vision, it is possible that there is no causal relationship at all between the strength of strategic vision and firm performance. Perhaps there is a third factor linked to both vision and performance, say, might be the *attitude towards technology* in the company. Firms that embrace computers and other technological advances may be the better performers in their industries because they are the first to exploit the new technologies (that is, "attitude towards technology" causes "performance"). As well, in highly computerized companies, there may be much more communication among employees–using electronic mail, visiting the company website and so on. Accessibility and sharing of information about the firm's strategies improves awareness and understanding of the vision among managers and employees (that is, "attitude towards technology" causes "vision"). So there may be neither a direct causal link or a reverse causal link between vision and performance, apart from the operation of this third factor, the attitude towards technology.

Another third factor could be having an innovative and charismatic CEO. An innovative CEO makes decisions before the firm's competitors do, creating competitive advantage and better firm performance. An innovative CEO makes changes that catch the attention of employees, who talk about the new ideas throughout the company, creating a strong vision. Again, there may be no direct link between vision and performance.

In summary, a correlation between two factors might be explained by one of three causal links. There may be a direct causal relationship, a reverse causal relationship or no relationship save through the effect of a third factor. Whenever an author describes a correlation and proposes a causal explanation for this correlation, as critical thinkers we must ponder the likelihood of reverse causation as well as the third factor effect.

Now think about this case: Strong entrepreneurial ambition, that is, desire to start one's own business, has been found to be associated with lower interest in higher education. Several business thinkers have discussed this inverse correlation, arguing that people who have an entrepreneurial personality are "hands-on," creative and risk-taking. Entrepreneurship is quite different from the world of higher learning, which tends to be structured, low-risk, and detached from the excitement of the real world of business. The stronger your entrepreneurial personality, then, the more likely you are to shun university, preferring to start your own company as early as possible. Can you come up with other possible causal explanations of this link?

The *post hoc ergo propter hoc* fallacy

An opinion piece in a community newspaper reads that: *Community policing came to our neighbourhood last summer. The police officers are now much more accessible than they were before; they ride around the streets on bicycles instead of patrol cars, they often wear shorts and look much more friendly than they used to. The new police station is much smaller than the old one and it looks more inviting—you can see plants in the windows and there is occasionally an open-house where the neighbours can go in and meet the policemen and women. This new strategy is very effective. I read in the newspaper recently that acts of vandalism and theft have decreased in the neighbourhood over the past 12 months. I know I feel much more comfortable when I am walking home from work this summer.*

The claim is that the community policing strategy has caused the decrease in crime. The reasoning appears to be that the police now have much more of a presence in the neighbourhood than used to be the case. Presumably, this increased visibility has discouraged would-be criminals, and so rates of criminal activity have gone down. But is this the only plausible explanation? It may be that the past 12 months have seen a high frequency of inclement weather–perhaps is has been colder, rainier or snowier than usual–and this has kept people at home and off the streets, both the potential criminals and the potential victims. In other words, unusual weather would have led to a drop in the crime rate, whether or not the policing strategy had changed. Here's another possibility: Economic conditions in the city have been brighter over the past year than they have been for quite some time. There have been announcements in the newspaper that the unemployment rate is decreasing. The house construction and renovation markets are enjoying a surge of activity. If more people are finding jobs and are thus better able to make ends meet, then this alone could have caused a drop in the crime rate, quite independently of the police officers' bicycles and open-house sessions.

Post hoc ergo propter hoc is a Latin phrase. Loosely translated it means: After this *(post hoc)* therefore *(ergo)* because of this *(propter hoc)*. *After* the new policing strategy was introduced, the crime rate decreased, *therefore* we assume that the decrease in crime must have occurred *because of* the strategy. This is a fallacy, an error in our reasoning. Just because an event was followed by another event, it does not necessarily mean that the first event caused the second.

Superstitious behaviour often has its root in the post hoc propter hoc fallacy. Some years ago, a student of mine came to an in-class test with a large key-ring in the shape of a rubber animal which he put on his desk. He had got the key-ring from his girlfriend the previous term, and happened to have it during a test he took. He did very well on the test, much better than he thought he would. Now the animal has become his test-taking mascot–always at his side to give him good luck. Having the animal and doing well on exams were associated in time, so he claims that the former caused the latter. I am certain that to a large extent, he was joking about this superstition, but it continues to affect his behaviour. Similarly, colleagues of mine have lucky ties, lucky pens, even a lucky restaurant in which to have lunch before a big presentation. All of these are claimed, tongue in cheek, to cause success at work. All started with events that were given a post-hoc-propter-hoc causal explanation.

Box 5-1: Charismatic leadership and task performance

What is the best kind of boss to have? One who inspires and excites you, one who helps you understand the details of the tasks to be done, or one who is friendly and concerned about your personal welfare? Business researchers label these three types of bosses as *charismatic* leaders, *structuring* leaders and *considerate* leaders respectively. Which of these three different leadership styles is best at motivating subordinates to work hard and effectively? Researchers Jane Howell, a professor at the University of Western Ontario, and Peter Frost, a professor at the University of British Columbia, conducted an **experiment** to examine this causal relationship between *leadership style* and *task performance*.

The research participants were 144 undergraduate business students at UBC who were each asked to play the role of a general manager dealing with a pile of items in his or her in-basket. The in-basket contained letters, reports and memos and the participants had to exercise their managerial judgement about how to handle each item—making decisions, delegating tasks, requesting further information and so on.

The task was presented to each student by a leader who used one of the three leadership styles. Although the participants did not realize it, the leader was actually an actor who had been carefully trained by the researchers to direct the work of the students using the three styles. As a *charismatic leader*, she presented an exciting goal, explaining how the task could foster links between the university and downtown businesses and would have a long term effect on the future commerce programs at UBC. Her tone was engaging, her body language was dynamic, and she expressed confidence that the participant would perform very well at the task. As a *considerate leader*, she was friendly and approachable, showing concern for

---

A friend of mine was called Rita throughout her childhood and adolescence. When she started working and moved out on her own, she changed her name to Catherine. "Rita is an unlucky name," she maintains. "My life was miserable until I changed my name, so I don't want anybody calling me Rita again, and bringing problems into my life." If we apply our critical thinking skills to my friend's causal reasoning, can we come up with plausible alternatives as to what, apart from her new name, may be causing her presently happy life?

the comfort and satisfaction of the participant. Her tone was warm; she leaned towards the participant, smiling and keeping eye contact. As a *structuring leader* she went through the directions point by point, explaining in detail how the task should be done and emphasised the standards of work performance. Her facial expressions and body language were neutral and business-like.

The participants were *randomly assigned* to one of the three experimental conditions. Apart from these differences in leadership style, however, they all worked in the same workroom, had the same in-basket exercise and were given the same length of time to work on the task. The leader always followed the same scripts and wore identical clothes—a dark, conservative business suit. By *controlling* these extraneous variables, the researchers were ensuring that the only difference between the three groups of participants was the leadership style they encountered. They can have confidence, therefore, that the level of performance achieved by the students can be attributed to the type of leadership style and nothing else.

So how did it turn out? You may be interested to know that the researchers found that charismatic leadership caused the best task performance. Participants who had the charismatic leader had the highest quality of work and suggested the most courses of action in the in-basket task. The other two styles caused similar, lower levels of performance. The researchers concluded that training leaders to be charismatic is not only possible, but desirable. The study needs to be repeated in a "real-life" work place, but on the basis of this experiment, it would appear that the boss's charisma causes high task performance in subordinates.

Howell, J. and Frost, P. (1989). A laboratory study of charismatic leadership, *Organizational behaviour and human decision processes*, *43*, 243-269.

Can we ever be sure?

We have shown that there are often multiple causes for an outcome. Whenever an author makes a causal claim, it is generally not difficult for the astute reader to come up with a rival cause that provides an equally good explanation for the outcome. It may be that the author's proposed cause is indeed the correct explanation. Any one of the plausible rival causes that occur to the critical reader may be the true interpretation.

Reflecting on Business *A handbook of critical thinking*

What is more, there may be *multiple causes*, that is, the correct explanation may involve more than one of these causal factors.

How, then, can we ever be sure about causal relationships? Can we ever rule out alternative causes and be confident that it is indeed one particular cause that leads to a given effect? Often it is important that we be sure of what is causing what. What would be the point of long hours spent working on our company's vision statement if this is not the true cause of business success? Why invest in all the changes necessary for community policing if we are not sure that our investments will really pay off in a low crime rate? In the applied, practical world of business, we have to be confident about causal relationships if we are to avoid wasting money and human effort.

Experimental research

Testing causal claims is the raison-d'etre of *experimental designs in business research*. The primary aim of an *experiment* is to rule out rival causal explanations. Experimental research designs increase our confidence in causal explanations. Here is an example of the simple experiment in business. Let's say that we want to know what is the best schedule for rest breaks for computer operators. Do they work most productively if they are given one hour for lunch, a 15-minute break in the morning and a 15-minute break in the afternoon? Would it be better to allow operators to vary the length and timing of the breaks however they please, as long as the total is 90 minutes? We call these two scenarios the 15-60-15 schedule and the 90-variable schedule. The next step is to separate the computer operators into two groups, each of which works to one of the two schedules. After a few work days, we compare the productivity of the two groups and find that the productivity of the 90-variable schedule operators is higher than the 15-60-15 operators. We conclude that having flexibility in rest breaks causes higher productivity.

You can see that it would be important to ensure that there are no differences between the two groups *other than* the different schedules. If for example, all the young computer operators were put in one group and all the older operators in the other, we would not know whether the productivity difference was due to age, schedule or both factors. Age would be a plausible alternative causal explanation. If one group had brand new computer equipment and the other group had older equipment, or if one group had a harder data-entry task than the other, differences in equipment or task difficulty would be plausible alternative explanations.

Researchers use a technique called *random assignment* to ensure that the characteristics of the people in different experimental groups are identical. With

62

random assignment every computer operator, whatever his/her age, gender, skill level, job tenure, etc, has an equal chance of being in either group. Researchers would also control variables such as task difficulty, pay levels, etc., keeping them as similar as possible across groups so they can rule out alternative causal explanations. Random assignment and control of extraneous variables help researcher to establish causal relationships with confidence. Box 5-1 presents another example of an experiment in business.

This is just a very brief introduction to experimental research. Close study of how to conduct valid experiments is beyond the purview of this handbook, but it is important to note that experimental research in business has become an essential tool in improving our understanding of business practice. In Box 5-2, you will find a description of a classic set of experiments in organizational research.

Formal experimentation can be costly and is not a tool that can be applied to every question. Intelligent, critical thinking, however, can be. As readers and managers, it is always important to be able to discern when an author has a strong, well-supported causal claim, and when the causal claims are contestable and open to many interpretations. In the latter case, when we recognise the existence of alternative causal explanations, we must use our logic to assess the *likelihood* of each possible cause. The most likely cause (or causes) will shape our overall evaluation of the author's claims and the seriousness with which we will take her argument.

Resource material for additional reading:
Chaffee, J. (1997). *Thinking critically*, 5th edition, Houghton Mifflin Co.
Sekaran, U. (1999). *Research methods for managers*, Wiley

Box 5-2: The Hawthorne experiments

The Hawthorne experiments were a series of large-scale experimental studies that formed an early milestone in the understanding of behaviour in organizations. Between 1924 and 1933, a group of investigators from the Harvard Business School conducted research studies at the Hawthorne plant of the Western Electric Company. The research was funded in part by manufacturers of electricity who wanted to show that higher levels of electrical lighting would cause improvements in industrial efficiency.

One of the studies employed two groups of workers whose average skill and productivity was the same. The first group worked under a constant illumination of 11 foot-candles. (A foot-candle is equal to the amount of light thrown by one candle on a square foot of a surface which is one foot away). The second group, the test group, were asked to work under progressively lower levels of light, going down to less than two foot-candles. The experimenters expected that the productivity of the test-group workers would decline as illumination got poorer. Instead, production increased in *both* groups. This increase in productivity was also found when the researchers changed other working conditions such as

---

Exercise 5-1: Causal thinking

Think about the following scenario: You arrive at the university library one Tuesday afternoon at 3 pm and find that the main doors are locked. What may be possible causes of this odd situation? Perhaps there was a gas leak or an electrical problem in the building and the library was closed down temporarily. Maybe it is a public holiday you'd forgotten about and the whole university is closed. There may be a problem with the doors and if you look carefully you'll see a sign telling you about an alternate entrance. Perhaps you're pushing instead of pulling, and the doors are not locked at all.

For most situations, there are a variety of causes that might explain a given effect. When an author proposes a particular causal relationship, the critical thinker must explore the plausibility of the causal link proposed, and decide whether there are other causes that are equally or more likely.

the length and frequency of rest periods and the length of the work day. When improvements in working conditions were taken away after several months, production continued to rise.

It appeared that whether lighting, work schedules and other working conditions were improved or made poorer, the productivity of the workers increased. In other words, any manipulation of working conditions, either for better or worse, improved productivity. The researchers concluded that variations in working conditions could *not* therefore be the *cause* of improved production. The cause seemed to lie in the fact that the workers who participated in the research were given *special attention* by the researchers and the plant managers. Getting special attention had been a much more powerful impetus to perform than any of the experimental conditions. This phenomenon has since been observed in innumerable experiments and has become known as the "Hawthorne effect."

Reference: Roethlisberger, F. and Dickson, W., (1966; c. 1939) *Management and the worker*, Harvard University Press

In the following exercise, use your creative powers by thinking of several possible causes for the given effects.

1. You've overslept three times in the past week.

2. Co-workers at your part-time job have suddenly stopped being friendly.

3. It takes you an hour to finish an exam that is scheduled to last for three hours.

4. Cars on a stretch of highway you drive every day seem to be going abnormally slowly.

5. Although overall industry sales are down, your product is exceeding projected sales figures.

6. Absenteeism in your department is higher in April than it was in March.

7. You didn't get the promotion you feel you deserved.

8. Every time you read your Marketing textbook, you start to feel sleepy.

9. One of your less talented subordinates is invited to lunch by your boss.

Part II: In each case, what sort of evidence would you need to see which of your causal explanations is most probable? Where would you find this evidence?

Exercise 5-2: Causal claims
In each of the passages below, identify the causal claim and the causal explanation offered. Can you think of a rival causal explanation? In other words, are there other plausible explanations for the relationship observed by the author? Draw on your understanding of differences between groups, association of characteristics and the post hoc fallacy to develop these rival explanations. Which of the explanations (including the author's) do you think is most likely?

1. In recent years, airline companies have banned cigarette smoking on flights. As a result, we have seen a substantial increase in incidents of "air rage" in which passengers become violent and abusive to airline staff as well as their fellow passengers. Nicotine deprivation causes passengers to become stressed and this is a major factor in air rage. The Canadian Council for Non-smoking wants airlines to make available nicotine-replacement products such as patches in order to stem the problem of air rage.

2. Over-achievers in the 1980s prided themselves on getting little sleep. In addition to long hours at the workplace, technological devices such as laptop computers, e-mail, voice-mail and the Internet make it possible to work into the wee hours of the night. Sleeping less meant they could work more and so be more successful. No longer. Sleep has become a new status symbol for successful executives. Jeff Bezos of Amazon.com, Marc Andreesen of Netscape Communications Corp, and Michael Bonsignore of Honeywell are just a few of the extremely successful top management executives who have found that getting eight hours of sleep each night leaves them refreshed, alert and creative. This increased mental acuity plays a major role in their success as executives. Today insufficient sleep is more characteristic of the less successful managers lower down the totem pole.

3. Progressive firms have "family friendly" policies, such as provisions for extended parental leave, the possibility of job-sharing, flexible hours, tele-commuting or on-site day care. This is more than just philanthropy–it makes good business sense. Employees in these firms can focus on getting their work done, secure in the knowledge that child care is well-managed, and that if a problem does arise, they will be able to get the time to deal with it effectively. Working for a firm that is not family friendly is considerably more stressful. In consequence, profitability is higher in a family-friendly firm.

4. My team mate, Noel, has said: "Whenever I dream about my old high school, the project on which I am currently working runs into problems. I experienced a lot of anxiety during high school and these dreams come like a sort of warning. Twice recently I had dreams about high school and look, our mark for this team project is only a C minus. It's not just superstition–this is how it turns out every time."

5. The role of the board of directors of a firm is to act in the shareholders' best interests, actively guiding the long-term management of the firm. In practice, board members may end up passively "rubber-stamping" top management decisions. Some scholars advocate that board members should be required to have significant stock ownership in the firm in order to ensure that they take an active interest. Research has found that the larger the stock holdings of a firm's board members, the more profitable the firm and the higher the share prices. This is because the share-holding board members have substantial stakes in the company's success. They are therefore more likely to look closely at the actions of management and make sure that managerial decisions are sound.

6. Daylight savings time is hazardous. The day after we move the clocks forward in the Spring, car accidents increase by 7%. This dramatic change is due to the loss of one hour's sleep. In the Fall, the day after we turn the clocks back and gain an hour's sleep, accidents decrease by 7%.

7. Many companies have recruitment programs that encourage current employees to refer outside applicants for job openings. In one such program at a large US bank, a review of over 5,500 job applications found that 35% of the people who were referred by employees were hired, while only 3% of the other applicants got jobs. The greater success of referrals comes because their friends provide inside information about when to present one's resume, the exact skills that are required for the job, and so on. Outsiders have little hope when competing against people with this privileged information from their personal connections. It really is who you know that counts in landing a job.

6 Techniques of persuasion

What makes an argument persuasive? How do authors convince readers to agree with their point of view? A variety of factors, several of which we have encountered in the earlier chapters, affect the persuasiveness of a text. Certainly the *quality of the evidence* presented for the claims is one such factor; we are persuaded when the evidence is accurate, precise, sufficient, representative, authoritative and clear. But just as it is essential to evaluate the evidence that is *presented*, it is equally important to think about the evidence that is *omitted*. Think, for example, of the possible reaction of an author who encounters a piece of evidence that contradicts his claim. In composing his text, he decides to omit several bits of data that are inconsistent with the conclusion that he wants to draw. As critical thinkers we must ask ourselves: What evidence gets left out because it is incompatible with the argument?

The *soundness of the causal argument* also makes a text persuasive. Yet it often happens that evidence presented may be compatible with more than one causal interpretation. When alternative causal explanations exist, this undermines confidence in the author's conclusion. For example, having found evidence of a strong relationship between A and B, the author might believe strongly that A caused B, but knows that another interpretation is that B caused A, a reverse causal explanation. How do writers deal most effectively with this problem of *rival explanations*?

Finally, we have seen that the extent to which the readers *agree with the underlying assumptions* of the writer plays an important role in their decision to accept or challenge the author's claims. *Conflicts in value preferences or reality assumptions* are common. How can an author be persuasive when her audience may not share her underlying beliefs or values?

The foregoing issues are related to the basic structure of an argument–claims, evidence and assumptions. A further aspect to be considered is the language and writing style used in the text. How does an author present her case most effectively, bringing her readers to appreciate fully the significance of her evidence? Do her words capture our attention and imagination, bringing her claims into clear (and persuasive) focus? In this chapter we shall also introduce *rhetoric*, which is the use of language to convince.

A "how-to" approach

The approach taken in this chapter is to describe *how to* build a persuasive argument, then we shall use this information to understand why certain authors are convincing and others not. We answer the questions posed above, deciding how to deal with contradictory evidence, alternative causal explanations and value conflicts, in a way that will be most persuasive to an audience. We take a brief look at effective use of words and other rhetorical devices which help us to present our claims most convincingly. Again, it must be stressed that we are *not* recommending that words be used as a smokescreen to conceal weak reasoning. As critical thinkers, we must always analyse the structure of the argument (claim, evidence & assumptions), however well or poorly the argument is worded. What we *are* advocating is clear and vivid writing that puts the reader in the author's shoes and allows him to live the experiences of the author or her sources.

The following sections discuss general strategies for building a persuasive argument. First we look at how to deal with objections to the structure of your argument. Next we focus on how to use language persuasively.

A theme that will come up repeatedly is the important requirement that you *think about your audience*. How much do your readers already know about the issue under discussion? How familiar might they be with the evidence you are about to present? Have they already formed their own ideas about the issue, and are they likely to agree or disagree with your claim? What might be the values that underlie their beliefs? Granted you rarely will know all these details about the beliefs and values of everyone who is likely to read your work. Further, you may have to write for a very diverse audience, making it more complicated to tailor your argument to a particular group. As we shall see, however, the more you think about your potential readers, the stronger the argument you can build. Forewarned is forearmed.

Anticipate and counter-argue readers' objections

The first step of writing persuasively is a brain-storming, trouble-shooting process in which you should put yourself in the shoes of your audience and perform "destructive testing" on your ideas. What objections could possibly be made to your argument? If your readers are fully-engaged, critical thinkers they will continually be consulting their own knowledge and beliefs, and will undoubtedly raise questions as they watch your reasoning develop. Recall that most interesting claims in the study of business tend to be *contestable* claims, so it is small wonder that they will be contested! If readers' objections are unaddressed in your writing, your claim will be dismissed out of hand. It follows that if you want to be persuasive, your job is to answer these expected questions as they arise. To do this you have to present the question or objection explicitly, then provide a convincing answer or rebuttal in your text. By mentioning and counter-arguing objections you will show your readers that you have considered the issue fully. If you *don't* address their concerns, they will simply think that it was your ignorance or naivete that led you to such a wrong-headed conclusion!

Some common types of objections that you can anticipate occur when: 1) Readers are aware of negative evidence that refutes your claim; 2) Readers can come up with alternative causal explanations that are consistent with your evidence; and 3) Readers disagree with your value preferences or reality assumptions.

Negative evidence The world is a complex and contradictory place, and it is rare that every piece of evidence that bears on an issue will lead irrevocably to a clear and unassailable conclusion. In fact, when they are doing research to support a claim, writers often have the experience of finding data and descriptions of events that run counter to the claim. So it should not be surprising that some readers are bound to think of disconfirming evidence that would undermine your argument. If you are aware of negative evidence, the sensible response is to present the negative evidence in order to show that you have given it due consideration. Thus you will show that, properly interpreted, it is not negative, or that it actually is not reliable. Consider how you might deal with very salient–and widely believed–evidence that contradicts your thesis about crime:

.... In summary, the crime rate is definitely on the decrease. Statistics from major cities across North America show this. However, when we read newspapers, watch television or go to the movies, it would appear that crime and violence are rampant. These reports cannot be disregarded. Crime news both on TV and in newspapers is much more explicit than it used to be; things that used to be passed over are now shown and described in full graphic detail. Movies that horrified people 20 years ago are just commonplace now. "Gangsta rap" is chic. Crime has become entertainment. But depictions of violence must not be mistaken for the phenomenon itself. Although it seems as if we are inundated with crime, this is quite misleading. The crime rate is indeed falling.

Or perhaps your claim is that successful entrepreneurs are very independent, but you know that there is a lot of focus on business networks as sources of advice for the entrepreneur. Again, you would mention the negative evidence and then show why it is misleading:

.... Many research surveys conclude that successful entrepreneurs have large networks of business colleagues and advisors. That, at least, is what the entrepreneurs say on paper-and-pencil questionnaires. But when we use a less superficial research technique, the in-depth interview, entrepreneurs go on to admit that they rarely use these networks for advice about business problems, and when they do, they find the advice they get is not particularly helpful. The networks may be there, but when it comes to advice about running the business, successful entrepreneurs make their own decisions and are fiercely independent.

Rival causes

If the claim you are proposing is a causal claim, it is likely that there are rival causal explanations of your evidence. Recall that plausible rival causes may be located in differences among groups, reverse causation, the effect of a third variable or the post hoc fallacy (see chapter 5 of this handbook). Certainly if you can think of a possible rival cause, it makes no sense to just keep quiet about the problem and hope the readers will not see the hole in your argument. It is guaranteed that some careful reader will catch the problem, especially if he or she disagrees with your claim. So as part of the brainstorming process, you must discipline yourself to find and propose alternative causes, then rebut them, showing the reader why they are unlikely to be the real explanation. For example:

> *All the firms we studied devoted a great deal of time and resources in managing relationships with their clientele. This relationship marketing was pivotal in ensuring their profitability. We considered the possibility that only profitable firms could afford to spend time focussing on relationship marketing. Could success have preceded their use of this marketing approach? A careful review of the history of each firm showed that the focus on client relationships generally came before they were successful. From the very beginning, the entrepreneurs emphasized the importance of getting to know the needs and personalities of their clients. It was not success, then, that caused this strategic approach. Rather, the strategy led to the ultimate success of the enterprise.*

As another example, consider how the systematic consideration and rejection of other explanations, anticipates the reader's questions about the causes of good course evaluations:

> *The students who were in small classes gave the course much higher ratings than the students in the large classes. Note that the time of day the course was held, the proportion of full-time and part-time students, and the average GPA of the students were all uncorrelated with the ratings. Moreover, most of the instructors taught both large and small sections so it was not the skill of the instructors that made the difference. We can conclude, therefore, that it was the small class size that caused students to be more enthusiastic about their courses.*

Debatable assumptions

In chapter 5 we discussed how critical thinkers can challenge underlying reality assumptions and values: first, they make the author's assumptions explicit, then they present counter-arguments to show that the assumptions are incorrect. To write persuasively, then, you must anticipate these challenges to your assumptions. If you know that there are reality assumptions that your audience might feel are debatable or wrong, you must provide explicit data to back up your assumptions. Here is an example:

*The series of workshops on stress relief for executives, organized by the Employee Assistance Program, has been a great success. A survey conducted by the HR department showed that workshop participants were enthusiastic about the sessions and reported that the stress-reduction techniques had a substantial positive impact on their performance on the job. Management should move quickly to make the program available to all employees. **Of course this assumes that lower-level employees could benefit from stress-reduction just as much as those at the executive level can. And there is no question that this assumption is warranted.** Studies show that first-line supervisors, sales representatives, secretaries–people in a variety of jobs–experience stress in this complex world of rapid change and uncertainty.*

Since stress, in the popular imagination, is often associated with high-powered, high-responsibility executive jobs, you have to anticipate that this reality assumption will lead some readers to disagree with your claim. So you deal with it explicitly, refuting the erroneous assumption with data.

When your readers' value preferences differ from your own, again your job is to show them that your value preferences are worth serious consideration. Although values can be resistant to change, it is also true that some value preferences may be just based on tradition or a feeling that "...well, doesn't everybody think the way I do?" Sometimes people have not actively questioned some of their values. If your writing poses a strong and logical challenge to their value assumptions, they may discover that they are not all that strongly committed to certain values. In cases like this, you do have a chance of persuading them to reflect on, and perhaps accept your viewpoint. Let's say, for example, that a reader believes an individual's right to privacy is important, but has not really thought carefully about what that might mean in a business context. You will need to anticipate this value conflict and your counter-argument will show the reader that the case for individual privacy is not clear-cut. Perhaps seeing your rationale might actually sway the reader to agree with your position.

Pzasz Executive Search has thorough and reliable head-hunting procedures. They are the consultants of choice for recruiting a senior administrator for our university. Their investigators research the accuracy of all resume items, follow up on all references and check with a variety of past co-workers about the candidate's credentials, character and integrity. They have even been known to question neighbours about the good citizenship of prospective administrators. Now some may feel that this close investigation invades the privacy of the individual. But let us balance the value of individual privacy against our responsibility to our institution. We need ethical leadership. Good moral character is demanded of teachers, police chiefs and heads of state. So too in university administrators. This person will represent our institution to the world, and must serve as a role-model for hundreds of academics and tens of thousands of students. Let us ensure that our choice is a good one.

Limit your claims when you have no rebuttal

And what of the objections that you can anticipate, but for which you cannot find a plausible rebuttal? It happens, even to the most practised researchers and writers. You must concede points that you cannot refute. This concession may take various forms.

1. Limits to your generalizations, as in: *All our evidence is drawn from large, high-tech corporations. Further research is necessary before we can confidently extend the claim to smaller firms, or those in other, more mature, industries.*

2. An assessment that the level of probability of your claim is less than 100%: *Although the evidence for my conclusion is mixed, it still is very probable that no-smoking regulations are a primary cause of air rage; the few contradictory cases are outweighed by far by the evidence that is consistent with my claim.*

3. A refinement or re-defining of your terms: *I've been arguing that when a CEO is promoted from within the organization, the company is more likely to be successful. Admittedly the hiring of outsider Michael Eisner as CEO of Walt Disney Inc. is a counter-example. However Eisner was carefully selected because he embodied all the vision and values of Disney. Researchers have quoted one manager as saying, "Eisner turned out to be more Walt than Walt." The key success factor, then, may be choosing a CEO who is committed to the values of the firm, **usually** someone who is promoted from within.*

Box 6-1: The rhetoric of textbooks

The world of business organizations is an unpredictable place. When we read the business news, work as employees in organizations, observe managers at work (see Box 2-1) or make decisions about our stock market investments, our impression of the business environment is characterized by ambiguity and uncertainty. Firms can be so fragile–here today and gone tomorrow. Managers may be "downsized"without warning. Technological advances, cultural diversity and globalization create constant change, unpredictability, even chaos in the world of business.

Yet how are business organizations portrayed in introductory business textbooks? Stephen Fineman and Yiannis Gabriel have pointed to an interesting gap between the unpredictability of today's organizations and the way in which these organizations are portrayed in introductory textbooks. The researchers studied textbooks in Organizational Behaviour, but their conclusions are probably applicable to textbooks in other disciplines of business. The standard textbook, Fineman and Gabriel argue, does not reflect our current understanding of business, but portrays organizations as structured, solid and stable. Their contention is that the *rhetoric of the textbook* makes this portrayal inevitable. The rhetorical devices commonly used in textbooks–definitions, case studies and lists–all make it appear that the information presented is factual, not contestable.

Definitions are usually highlighted or placed in boxes or margins for emphasis. Definitions convey the idea of science, precision and rigour. They represent a conveniently-sized piece of information that can be memorized and reproduced in examinations and reports. By their very nature, definitions encourage students to accept the information presented as indisputable facts.

It may seem to you that making these concessions and describing limitations to the truth of your claims weakens your argument. Actually it does just the opposite. It is paradoxical but true that *acknowledging limitations makes your writing more persuasive.* By considering the full complexity and nuance of the claim, you show

Case studies are often used in textbooks to illustrate concepts. It might seem that case studies can demonstrate the chaos and unpredictability of "real life." Typically they do not. The "characters, plots and narrative are condensed, reduced to a minimalist state ... [which serves to] reinforce the image of organizations as orderly and impersonal (p. 382-3)."

Lists aid memorization but eliminate argument. Authors rarely present their arguments for the inclusion or exclusion of elements on the list. Too often, learning comes to mean associating a list of authors' names with theories, and each theorist with a list of key terms.

In general then, the definitions, case studies and lists that are characteristic of textbooks leave the reader with the impression that the facts are clear. The effect of these devices is practically to eliminate critical thought, argument and debate.

Buying an introductory textbook is a part of "rite of passage" into a discipline that is new to the student. Since it is establishing the discipline in the student's mind, the emphasis is on what is known, on the power of the discipline. Everything seems clear-cut and well understood. "The textbook is a ticket to a club, a fount of knowledge and a guarantee of safe passage" (p.379). Issues that raise too many questions are necessarily excluded as inviting unwanted ambiguities. As a result, the turbulence that characterizes the real world of organizations vanishes, and the reader is left with an inaccurate picture of organizational stability and orderliness.

Fineman, Stephen and Gabriel, Yiannis (1994). Paradigms of organizations: An exploration in textbook rhetorics, *Organization*, 1 (2), 375-399, Sage.

yourself to be thoughtful and judicious. Readers can see that you have weighed pros and cons and used your critical powers of judgement to come up with a conclusion. If an author just presents a "bare-bones" claim-and-evidence text, her argument often seems naive, if not downright simple-minded.

Rhetoric

In this section we consider how the use of language affects the credibility and persuasiveness of your argument. Language is the primary tool to communicate thinking. One of the attributes that sets human beings apart from other animals is our ability to convey complex, abstract or personal experiences to other human beings through speech, reading and writing. Some writers know how to use language well; others are sloppy, imprecise and therefore unconvincing. Some people are good at conveying emotions with their words–they create in their readers and listeners feelings of anger, pride, indignation, fear, etc. The study of style and persuasion using language is known as *rhetoric*. We study rhetoric to understand the techniques used by authors and speakers to convince an audience of the rightness of their views. Box 6-1 provides an analysis of the rhetoric commonly used by textbook writers.

You may have heard people speak disparagingly of rhetoric, often when using the phrase, "empty rhetoric." In this construction, rhetoric means the use of language that is artificial, elaborate and showy, with very little real substance to the arguments it is intended to support. Rhetoric in this sense usually involves a deliberate intent to mislead. There is a vast public relations industry whose major task is to ensure that the information that people get about the corporate world is presented in the best possible light (see Box 6-2). It is unfortunate that language can be used to manipulate readers and conceal insincerity, but it should be equally obvious that not all people who use words effectively are hypocrites. People also use language to convey sincerely-held opinions, to inform, enlighten and share their human experiences. The existence of spin doctors should not lead to a cynical rejection of rhetoric. Most students of rhetoric are people who want to convey their ideas as clearly and accurately as possible.

Here follows a brief overview of some of the rules of rhetoric.

Be complete

The first rule is that you must present your reasoning in full and clear detail. As a beginner in business writing, you may not realize that much of the evidence you present will be new to the reader. The world of business is vast, and a multitude of issues and events is subsumed under the heading of business studies. Even experienced managers and business scholars cannot keep track of it all. It is important to frame your writing with sufficient points of content to allow potential readers to make the connection to his or her own experience. Moreover you will have spent a lot more time thinking about your particular argument than most of your readers. You have worked hard to collect evidence and to organise it into a coherent position. Use your evidence thoroughly–to its maximal potential. This does not mean a painstaking reconstruction of all your initial mistaken thoughts, your difficulties in finding reliable evidence, or all the blind alleys you ran into as you developed your ideas. But do give enough detail (within your space or time restrictions) to allow your audience a full appreciation of the import of your data and logic. Undeveloped ideas and an assumption that your audience will "fill in the blanks," are not persuasive.

Box 6-2: Press releases and the business news

Where do newspaper reporters get information for their articles? A substantial portion of the business information we read in newspapers comes from **press releases** written by the firms themselves and transported, holus bolus, into the news articles. **Press conferences** are often called when major firms are changing their leadership or introducing new products. As we might expect, the information presented to the news media in press releases and at press conferences is carefully worded by skilled public relations professionals to make the firm look efficient, progressive and successful. They are written to produce what PR specialists have termed "good ink." So to the extent that rushed and harried reporters rely on the information and even the wording of press releases (conveniently crafted for this purpose), it may be unwise to expect that articles reported in newspapers are unbiased facts. There's another factor that creates bias in business reporting. Too much bad press might lead companies to withdraw their advertisements, and corporate advertisements are an important source of revenue for newspapers. For most newspapers, advertisements typically bring in much more revenue than individual and subscription sales of the newspaper to readers. It is little wonder that the news is full of flattering stories and glowing reports about business.

Use an appropriate tone

When you write you create a relationship between yourself and your eventual audience. This relationship may be quite formal and distant, or may have a more informal and personal quality. The quality of the writer/reader relationship that is inherent in your writing is known as *tone*. By thinking of your future readers, you can decide whether a formal, *scholarly* tone or a less formal *narrative* tone would be more appropriate.

The scholarly tone is characterised by rational exposition of the structure of your argument. Logic is highly prized. The scholarly tone uses formal, technical language or abstract analysis, and makes frequent reference to the ideas of academic experts

---

Box 6-3: Marketing myopia and the power of rhetoric

Theodore Levitt, a professor of marketing, wrote an extremely popular article in a 1960 issue of the *Harvard Business Review*.[1] Levitt's major claim was that firms should think of themselves, not in terms of the particular product or service they offer, but in terms of the broad industry within which the product or service is located. Railways, for example, should define themselves as operating in the transportation industry; oil companies are in the energy business. This broader focus will ensure companies' continued growth, even in the face of technological change. Why? Because transportation will always be necessary, even if rail travel is eroded by growing use of cars, airplanes and trucks. As all particular products (and services) are bound to be obsolete eventually, a *product* orientation is therefore myopic. A *customer* orientation, on the other hand, offers more growth opportunity in an environment of technological change. Firms that focus heavily on production methods, and on product research and development, but ignore customers and markets are said to be suffering from **marketing myopia** and are destined for obsolescence.

Levitt's article was enormously influential. His ideas were put into practice by airlines, publishing houses, car companies, oil companies, shoe stores and cosmetic firms among others. In the first fifteen years after its publication, *Harvard Business Review* sold over a quarter of a million reprints of the article. The results of implementing these ideas have been mixed. Some firms benefited greatly from this heightened awareness of the market in which they operated, but some others ended up defining themselves so broadly that they lost focus and diversified into inappropriate areas. In the words of one of Levitt's critics,[2] "Why should a few clever words on a piece of paper enable a railroad company to fly airplanes, or for that matter, run taxicabs? (p. 280)."

---

and researchers in the field. Academic journals and most textbooks are written in this way. Citations, footnotes and reference lists are standard. In some areas of business, scholarly writing is very mathematical. Essentially, the scholarly tone is an *appeal to authority*.

In a retrospective commentary, Levitt pondered the astounding impact of his article: "Why its appeal throughout the world of resolutely restrained scholars, implacably temperate managers and high government officials, all accustomed to balanced and thoughtful calculation? Is it that concrete examples, joined to illustrate a simple idea and presented with some attention to literacy, communicate better than massive analytical reasoning that reads as though it were translated from the German? Is it that provocative assertions are more memorable and persuasive than restrained and balanced explanations, no matter who the audience? (p. 14)."

Levitt is suggesting that it was primarily the **rhetorical quality** of his article that accounted for its success, in particular, his use of a strong **narrative tone**. The article is full of vivid, colourful examples of Hollywood movie producers, the first supermarkets, the self-limiting strategies of oil companies and car manufacturers. He makes dramatic over-statements of his case, suggesting, for example, that product-oriented engineers in R&D see customers as "unpredictable, varied, fickle, stupid, shortsighted, stubborn, and generally bothersome." He describes a Boston millionaire who declared that his entire estate should be invested solely and forever in streetcars, because of his myopic belief that this product would always be in demand. He mentions John Rockefeller creating a market by sending free kerosene lamps to China. These and other examples combine to grab the readers' attention and make his article very convincing.

1. Levitt, T. (1975). Marketing myopia, *Harvard Business Review*, Reprint of 1960 article.
2. Mintzberg, H. (1994). *The rise and fall of strategic planning*, Free Press, New York.

The narrative tone is characterized by stories and anecdotes. Vividness is emphasized. The writer uses many descriptions and examples, sometimes including actual quotations from managers, customers, consultants, etc. where they are relevant to the argument. Striking personal experiences, first-hand observations and dramatic case-studies are frequent when writers use a narrative tone. Business newspapers and magazines, as well as popular trade books in business tend to use this tone (see Box 6-3). The narrative tone often entails an *appeal to emotion*.

Selecting your tone means thinking about your audience. Publishers usually know who their main audience is, and business authors choose their tone depending on where their work will be published. As a business student, you probably should aim for a middle ground in your writing. You will want to demonstrate to your teachers that you are becoming increasingly familiar with the work of scholars in your field of study. At the same time, business studies is an *applied* field and it is equally important that you learn to write for an audience of business practitioners who might be suspicious of or bored by a strictly academic style. As will be argued in the next section, even the most analytical, matter-of-fact of texts can profit from vividness and detail if the author wants to be convincing.

Be vivid

By using vivid language, you bring your evidence to life, attracting attention to your points and making them memorable for your readers. In this section we shall mention a few techniques that are commonly used to make writing more vivid, and therefore more persuasive. These brief pointers, however, are no substitute for a good guidebook on writing style. Countless style guides exist which are invaluable aids for the beginning as well as the experienced writer. Find one you like and use it regularly.

As you read the following report from an employee newsletter, ask yourself whether vivid images of the event and its impact on the employees' morale spring to mind.

> *The meeting was well-attended and pretty interesting. The division manager said that profits were low last quarter and people were not too happy, but a new supplier has made a good offer to provide raw material at a more reasonable cost and there is a window of opportunity to bring in some high-tech equipment soon. This means that by next year things should be better in the division, especially if there is belt-tightening in other areas, so by the end of the meeting people felt pretty good about that.*

Why is this piece not vivid? First, there are many **vague words**, words that are imprecise and do not stimulate readers' imaginations. "Interesting," "low," "reasonable" and "pretty good" are vague. In the paragraph, few **concrete details** are provided to make the incident memorable. Metaphorical phrases like "window of opportunity" and "belt-tightening," which may once have been vivid, have been so over-used in business writing that they are now listless **cliches**. Now we rewrite the text, replacing vague words more precise ones, providing concrete details of the setting of the meeting and the actual words of the participants, all of which are designed to bring the event to life for the readers. Fresher, more vigorous phrases take the place of the cliches.

> *Practically the entire department attended the open meeting, which was originally scheduled to meet in the departmental training room. Because of the unprecedented numbers the meeting had to be moved to the board room. The extraordinary interest was a result of last month's financial results: profits had plummeted from $460,000 a month to just over $135,000. What had gone wrong? Who was to blame? Anxiety levels were high.*
>
> *The fundamental problem according to Bert Sheldon, the manager, was skyrocketing raw material costs. Lupu Inc., the regular supplier, had changed its pricing policy with scarcely any notice. That together with a tightening supply market caused raw material costs to go up 22%, all but wiping out profit. He had remonstrated with Lupu at the highest level but to no avail. So two decades of working with Lupu ended in a call for bids. A new arrangement now exists with Playfair & Long who, in exchange for an exclusive contract, will supply us at 5% less than the spot rate on the London Metal Exchange. Moreover, P & L can supply and install high tech sealant machines which, in the long run, should reduce operating costs by 2 to 3 percent. Initial financing costs are hurting, but with a sharp eye kept on other costs, strong performance is expected within a year.*
>
> *The meeting left employees with a clear signal that head office has the situation firmly in hand. The initial glum atmosphere was entirely dispelled and optimism reigned.*

Rewritten, the text is considerably longer, but much easier to visualize. The use of precise, vivid language convinces the reader of the importance of the meeting and conveys clearly the shift in morale among the employees. Again, it cannot be emphasized enough that almost all writers rely on dictionaries, thesauruses and style guides to help them seek appropriate words and phrases, to ensure correct usage and to rise above vagueness and cliche.

Effective reading

The intelligent use of rhetoric, then, goes hand in hand with the development of a sound, logical argument. Neither aspect is sufficient by itself. By analogy, when you have cooked a delicious meal, you want to be sure to serve it on a clean plate with an attractive table setting. It detracts greatly from good food if it is served on dirty dishes or in unappetising surroundings. Everyone appreciates a skilful wordsmith, but if your argument is not sound and you try to cover up its deficiencies with emotional or authoritative language, then you are encouraging fallacious thinking. As a writer, you must make every effort to ensure that there is substance underlying your well-crafted prose.

You cannot assume, however, that all writers marry a sound argument with persuasive writing. It sometimes happens that an author's excellent command of rhetoric is accompanied by a weak argument structure. As a critical reader your first task is to expose and criticize the bare bones of the argument–the claims, evidence and assumptions, independently of the rhetorical devices that the author added for impact and readability.

And consider the other possibility. Occasionally you will encounter a writer who has a poor command of language and style. Try not to be distracted; invaluable ideas may often be found in unappealing packages. Again, by focussing on claims, evidence and assumptions, you may find that the awkward prose conceals a treasure trove of intellectually stimulating information.

Resource material for additional reading:

Browne, N. & Keeley, S. (1994). *Asking the right questions*, Prentice Hall.
Ruggiero, V. (1998). *The art of thinking,* 5th edition, Longman.

Exercise 6-1: Vague words

"A *middle-aged* acquaintance of mine recently decided to leave a *high-paying* job in a *large city* to take instead a *low-paying* job in a *small town*."

Replace each of the italicized words with a precise number that seems appropriate:

middle-aged	=	_____	years old
high-paying	=	$_____	as an annual salary
large city	=	_____	residents
low-paying	=	$_____	as an annual salary
small town	=	_____	residents

Part II: Ask five other people to do this exercise. Try to find people of varying ages and backgrounds. Compare the answers you get.

Exercise 6-2: Removing rhetorical flourishes
Read the following passage and rewrite it using simple, factual prose. Eliminate emotional language, the colourful phrases, and the rhetorical devices that are intended to persuade the reader. Thereafter, compare the original to your rewrite. What is your reaction to the differences?

Productivity problems? What company is immune? When your personnel costs are high, even small improvements in your workers' efficiency can make a big difference to your beleaguered bottom line. Professor Kevin Warwick, a leading researcher in cybernetics at Reading University in England, may have the answer–in a tiny silicon chip.

Prof. Warwick's cutting-edge research made headline news in the summer of 1998 when the intrepid scientist arranged to have a silicon chip implanted in his own arm. He demonstrated that all his movements could then be monitored on a computer, via receptors which were located at various positions in the building where he worked. Subsequent tests on other volunteers have allowed him to perfect this technique of tracking the whereabouts of individuals as they wander about designated buildings.

Reflecting on Business *A handbook of critical thinking*

As a measure of timekeeping and efficiency, the business potential of this scientific breakthrough is exciting. And at a cost of just a few dollars per employee, improved productivity is rarely to be had so cheaply. According to the *London Times*, Prof. Warwick has been approached by several firms who are eager to learn more about this new technology.

Part II
Rewrite the passage once more, this time from the point of view of someone who wants to persuade the reader that this is a dangerous innovation.

Overview & Comprehensive Exercises

In this final section, we review the major principles outlined in this handbook. The review is followed by a series of comprehensive exercises which you can use to practice your critical thinking skills.

The three major components of an argument[1]

Claim Major conclusion of a piece of writing which summarizes the author's position

Evidence Examples, reasons, statistics, anecdotes or previously-established claims that provide support for the claim.

Underlying assumptions General statements that establish the link between the evidence and the claim.

Counter-arguments may exist because of negative evidence, alternative causal explanations, or challenges to the author's underlying assumptions.

Claim

Women are more successful on the stock market than men.

Evidence

Studies show that the average male investor got a 1.4% lower return than the average woman over a 6-year period. Female investment fund managers also performed better than their male counterparts. This is because men are over-confident and make trades too often.

Underlying assumption

We take it for granted that percent returns is a good indicator of successful investment.

Counterargument

It must be acknowledged, however, that mediocre women are less likely to survive in the investment arena than mediocre men, so possibly it is expertise rather than gender per se that is creating the difference.

[1]The example in the diagram is drawn from Bell, A. (1999) I am woman, watch my stocks soar, *Globe and Mail*, 17 April, B6.

Writing a persuasive essay

1.   Be clear in your own mind about what your claim is. Make sure that you do enough reading and thinking about the issue so you know that your claim is defensible. Concept maps can be helpful in summarizing complex claims for your readers.

2.   Outline the evidence for your claim. Use your sources well to ensure that your evidence is authoritative and accurate. Statistics and direct quotes improve the precision of your writing. Get a great enough variety of sources of evidence to achieve sufficiency and representativeness.

3.   Ensure that the evidence you select is relevant. What underlying assumptions lead you to choose these particular pieces of evidence? Are your assumptions so generally accepted that they can remain implicit, or do you need to state them explicitly?

4.   Anticipate that at least some readers will have objections that may be related to conflicting assumptions and values, alternative causal explanations or other problems with your evidence. Deal with these potential objections explicitly by rebutting them or limiting your argument.

5.   Present your ideas as clearly and vividly as possible. After you have written your first draft, re-read it and make revisions. Have a friend read your work and make changes based on his or her input.

Critical Reading

Underline the words that locate claims and evidence, words that catch your attention because they are surprising, arouse emotion, are ambiguous, etc.

Annotate the text with your own comments in the margins

> Examine the quality of the evidence: sufficiency, accuracy, precision, representativeness, authority and clarity. Make a note when any aspect of quality strikes you as particularly good or bad.

> Make the author's assumptions explicit. If there are reality or value assumptions that you want to challenge, make a note of it.

> Consider the author's rhetorical style. How has he or she used words to increase the persuasiveness of the piece?

> Write down any questions, counterarguments or supporting evidence that occur to you as you read.

Consider the components of the author's argument in light of your own prior beliefs and values. Did you initially agree or disagree with the author's claim? How might this have affected your reading? What do you believe now?

Overleaf is an example of the **first steps** of such an analysis, applied to an excerpt from an interview with a Montreal entrepreneur (names and some details have been changed to protect his anonymity). Notice the reader's marginal comments and how his reaction changes from the beginning to the end of the piece. Which comments are related to his analysis of the qualities of the evidence? Which are related to underlying assumptions? What are your own reactions? Are they similar to or different from this reader's?

Claim is in opening (and closing) sentences	Family members in the business is a big no-no. The smart entrepreneur will keep his family as far away from the business as possible. Believe me, I've been 36 years in	*Lots of experience which increases authority. Must be a pretty old guy!*

Claim is in opening (and closing) sentences

Cue words for evidence #1

Family members in the business is a big no-no. The smart entrepreneur will keep his family as far away from the business as possible. Believe me, I've been 36 years in business and I've been burned often. For example I had my ex-wife's sister running my store in the west end. You'd figure this would be someone I could trust, but all I got from her was headaches. Sometimes it was ten o'clock, ten thirty, eleven o'clock, she's not there yet to open the store. I was losing money hand over fist, and in the end, I had to fire her and close the store. As you can imagine, it didn't make me too popular. But what else could I do?

Lots of experience which increases authority. Must be a pretty old guy!

Anecdotal evidence. Vivid narrative style makes it clear and easy to read

Evidence #2

Assumption that lots of time spent with spouse is a negative outcome. What a jerk! No wonder they're divorced.

And that wasn't all. Back in the eighties, my wife was working as my bookkeeper at the downtown store. We'd be together all day long, we'd be eating breakfast, lunch and dinner together, we'd come to work together and go home together. Ninety-five percent of my waking hours were with that woman. It was all too much.

Evidence #3

Implicit assumption that the son is not interested in work.

It's not just wives–all your family take you for granted. Take Victor, a buddy of mine who has a property management business. He worked long, hard hours, nurturing this little business so that finally he made something great out of it. Then he brings his son on board. Big mistake. According to Victor, all the kid wants is to draw a big salary. He sees his father driving a Lexus, he wants one too. He wants to be a chief without ever having been an Indian. What he doesn't understand is that his father has paid his dues. You've got to earn it.

Another anecdote. Is this generalizable?

Phrase evokes sympathy for Victor

Is this racist? I'm not sure, but I don't think I like this guy!

Evidence #4

Evidence #5

Survey is more precise and authoritative than anecdotes

Look at the Eatons. Look at the McCain family. And remember the Steinbergs? Everywhere you look you see family businesses in trouble or going down the tubes. It's not just my opinion. Experts agree that working with family members is a problem. A survey done by a couple of professors in a Montreal business school showed that 54% of the entrepreneurs they interviewed said that working with family members creates problems. Business is business. Right or wrong, you are not your brother's keeper. Family and business don't mix.

I can think of other family businesses that contine to be successful. The Bronfmans, the Saputos, my friend Diana's in-laws.

How many entrepreneurs did they interview? Is 54% high enough for me to buy this evidence? If he'd given the names of the profs it would be more persuasive.

The phrase makes it sound like he's not really interested in considering any opposing viewpoint. The whole thing is pretty one-sided.

Comprehensive Exercise #1
Hi-tech CEOs Say Value of Liberal Arts is Increasing

TORONTO, April 7 /CNW/ - Funding of higher education in this country needn't be an either/or proposition between technology or liberal arts and sciences, as public debate suggests.

As leaders of some of Canada's growing high-technology companies, we have first-hand knowledge of the necessity for a balanced approach.

Yes, this country needs more technology graduates, as they fuel the digital economy. But it is impossible to operate an effective corporation in our new economy by employing technology graduates alone. We have an equally strong need for those with a broader background who can work in tandem with technical specialists, helping create and manage the corporate environment.

A liberal arts and science education nurtures skills and talents increasingly valued by modern corporations. Our companies function in a state of constant flux. To prosper we need creative thinkers at all levels of the enterprise who are comfortable dealing with decisions in the bigger context. They must be able to communicate–to reason, create, write and speak–for shared purposes: For hiring, training, managing, marketing, and policy-making. In short, they provide leadership.

For example, many of our technology workers began their higher education in the humanities, and they are clearly the stronger for it. This was time well spent, not squandered. They have increased their value to our companies, our economy, our culture, and themselves, by acquiring the level of cultural and civic literacy that the humanities offer.

We stand with the chancellors of Ontario's universities, who recently stated that funding must "permit universities to manage enrolment demand and maintain a diverse and forward-looking curriculum."

It is critical that all universities in Canada receive sufficient funding to ensure a well-educated workforce and a new generation of leadership.

Pierre-Paul Allard, President and Managing Director, Cisco Systems Canada Co.
Paul Bates, President and CEO, Charles Schwab Canada, Co.
Everett Anstey, President, CEO and Chairman ,Sun Microsystems of Canada
Kevin Bennis, President and CEO, Call-Net Enterprises Inc. (Sprint Canada)
Micheline Bouchard, Chairman, President and CEO, Motorola Canada Co.
Jean Monty, President, and CEO, BCE Inc.

Paul Butler, Director, Artech Digital Entertainments
Michael O'Neil, Country Manager, International Data Corporation
Stuart Butts, Chairman and CEO, Xenos Group Inc.
Joseph Pilarski, CEO and Director, EcomPark Inc.
Peter Ciceri, President and Managing Director, Compaq Canada Inc.
Eugene Polistuk, President and CEO, Celestica Inc.
Ashraf Dimitri, President, Oasis Technology Ltd.
Doug Steiner, CEO, Versus Technologies Inc. (E*Trade)
Kevin Francis, Chairman, President and CEO, Xerox Canada Inc.
Carol Stephenson, President and CEO, Lucent Technologies Canada
James de Gaspé Bonar, President and CEO, CCH Canadian Limited
Guthrie Stewart, Executive Vice President, Global Development, Teleglobe Inc.
Grant Gisel, President, Sierra Systems Group Inc.
Don Tapscott, President and CEO, New Paradigm Learning Corporation
Carl Glaeser, CEO, Bowne Internet Solutions
Yves Thibodeau, President, Canadian Division, DMR Consulting Inc.
Dean Hopkins, CEO, Cyberplex Interactive Media.
David Ticoll, Managing Director and CEO, Alliance for Converging Technologies
Robert Johnson, CEO and President, Bowne & Co. Inc
Sheelagh Whittaker, President and CEO, EDS Canada Inc
Paul Tsaparis, President and CEO, Hewlett-Packard (Canada) Ltd.
D. Craig Young, Vice Chairman and President, AT&T Canada Inc
David Wagner, President and CEO, Unisys Canada Inc
John Wetmore, President and CEO, IBM Canada Ltd.

www.newswire.ca/releases/april2000/07/c1770.html [Accessed 10 April 2000]

Comprehensive Exercise #2
Casual Dress Days
This piece was written by a bank employee who wishes to remain anonymous.

How do you dress for success? The received wisdom was that men wore business suits and ties in sombre colours, while women were counselled to wear skirts and blazers, eschewing frills. A few years back there was a slight relaxation in the dress code–Casual Fridays came to the Bank where I work. This meant slacks and sombre v-neck sweaters at the end of the week, like we just stepped out of a GAP commercial. Then a few days ago, the chairman announced a major policy change. Now every day is Casual Dress Day.

Apparently, the guys in the executive suite want to shed the tired old image of us bankers being up-tight, conservative business men in blue pin-stripe suits. The idea seems to be that we should be more like those dot-com corporate clients of ours. The techies with long hair, khaki pants, and lots of attitude. They want to project the new image of our Bank—no longer a custodian of cash and coin, but of information. Our casual wear is supposed to reflect a new generation of workers who live in a wired world, relying on Palm Pilots, digital cellular phones, credit and debit cards, fax machines, laptop computers, e-mail, voice mail, remote garage door openers, pagers, microwave ovens, DVD players and 1-800 pizza delivery. Our new 21st century image is "computer nerd."

When I started to work for the Bank, my sartorial options were limited and life was simple. I had five nice suits and wore one each day of the week. I just spent a thousand dollars last year on a couple of new suits. Now I they want me to buy a whole new wardrobe to keep up with the times! But maybe I'll fix those bastards and wear the same five suits I always did. I'll be the office rebel. The rebel in a suit and tie!

Because I'm not sure I follow the logic here. How does forcing me to abandon my suits and ties for chinos and polo shirts change me? I'm still the same person inside, and the dot-com techies would be nuts if they didn't know it. Yet I see reports in the newspaper that with this dress policy our bank is "getting in touch with its high tech clients and the new world out there." Another PR type was burbling on that "we really feel we have to adapt" to the changes in the business dress of our clients. I don't get it. Can anyone explain to me how this is supposed to work?

Comprehensive Exercise #3
The Toco Port and Ferry Service

The Government of Trinidad and Tobago, a two-island republic in the southern Caribbean, recently announced plans to establish a new ferry service. The ferry will run between Tobago, the smaller island which is 30 miles north-east of Trinidad, and Toco, a small coastal village on the north-eastern tip of Trinidad. The current stage of the project is that a developer has been selected, and all that remains is to negotiate the terms of a final agreement. This proposed development, if it goes ahead, will replace the current ferry service between Tobago and the capital city of Port of Spain, which is on the island of Trinidad. It will also radically change economic, social and environmental life in the Toco region. As such, it must be very carefully considered, with the involvement of the widest possible range of stakeholders in the debate.

The village of Toco lies in a pristine natural setting. Rainforests stretch into the hills to the west and south. Many residents cultivate small agricultural plots in the forests, providing subsistence and a basic income. The ocean beyond, the meeting point of the Caribbean Sea and the Atlantic Ocean, is the site of Trinidad's only coral reef. Fishing is a major source of livelihood in the community, though declining fish stocks and the threat posed by large commercial fishing interests are an ever-present problem for the small fishermen. In recent years, eco-tourism has been a growing alternative to farming and fishing, the traditional methods of generating income. Nesting grounds for the giant marine leatherback turtles, the nearby beaches have great potential as an eco-tourist destination.

How does the proposed port and ferry service fit in this picture? Evidence from use statistics of the existing ferry from Port of Spain indicates that the ferry is used primarily by Tobagonians who are travelling to and from Trinidad to transact business–they are market vendors, building contractors, hardware dealers, and other business people shopping for consumer goods and building materials. Relocating this service in Toco will require a dredged harbour, a jetty, parking for a large number of cars, trucks and containers, turn around facilities, warehouses and hotels. Almost all the ferry traffic, passengers and freight, will be going to and from Port of Spain. Toco is currently a two-hour drive from Port of Spain, mainly along a narrow, winding coastal road. Miles of wider roadway will have to be built to accommodate trailer trucks and much heavier traffic. All of these developments will utterly change the face of Toco and the surrounding region.

The plan envisages reclaiming from the sea two to three hectares of land on which these facilities will be built. What will be the impact of this land reclamation on the fragile reef system? How will the diverted sea water be handled in order to avoid coastal erosion, flooding or the salination of rivers? What are the plans to manage industrial effluent and other pollutants? There is no evidence that environmental impact studies are being carried out. In any case, there are many examples which prove that government watchdog agencies lack the "teeth" to curb the excesses of commercial interests. How is this apparently lackadaisical attitude consistent with Toco's emerging eco-tourism activities?

Other outcomes must also be considered. Many farmers in Toco cultivate ancestral lands for which no property deeds exist. With the proposed developments, land values are sure to rise. What will be the protection for these deed-less farmers from unscrupulous land speculators? We can learn a lesson from Tobago here–with the large-scale development of tourism in the past two decades, many residents of the island of Tobago have found themselves marginalised, no longer able to afford the escalated property values that came with the influx of European and North American currency.

Should the ferry project go ahead, a rise in population is to be expected, and there will be a severe strain placed on existing health and social services, public utilities, schools, policing, transport and other community facilities. Currently, many of these services are close to primitive; substantial improvement will be necessary if the proposal goes through. Yet in a meeting with a Toco community leader, the Minister of Works declared that private commercial interests will be funding the project entirely, and "the government will not be spending a cent." This statement, meant as an assurance, is cause for alarm. Moreover the government negotiating team that is responsible for the final agreement with the developer, has no representatives from the Toco community.

No doubt the building of the facility will provide employment for young people, most probably as labourers. While this may seem advantageous, it is definitely a short-term benefit. Once the facility is complete, labour needs will be for skilled workers, and few of the Toco workers will be able to compete for these jobs. Chances are, however, that they will be reluctant to return to fishing and farming. And even if they are interested in returning to their old lifestyles, they may find that their land has been expropriated and that fishing is less viable than it was. The government has stated that longer-range plans for the region include the building of a heliport, bunkering facilities for gas and oil, a marina for pleasure craft and a cruise ship terminal. Clearly, little thought has been given to the needs of the community. Preferred development would be in ecologically-aware, small-scale industries that draw on local skills and the available natural resources to create long-term employment and economic development. Such industries might include the manufacture of paper, rope, woven mats and brooms from the native grasses, pottery products made from available clays and sand, and a variety of organic products such as fertilizers and animal feed (from seaweed), and spices, herbal preparations and cosmetics (from the varied plant life that is abundant in the area). Heliports and cruise ships are not harmonious with Toco village life.

In a community newsletter, Edward Hernandez, the curator of a Tobago museum noted that the social impact of rapid development in Tobago has included a rise in theft and crimes against persons, drug trafficking and drug use, and an increase in prostitution, sexually-transmitted diseases and mental health problems. In conclusion, it is vital that we learn from the lessons of recent history and reconsider this ferry project. Development, yes. But development that empowers the local community, preserves the natural environment and allows the people of Toco a viable future.

The author thanks the curators of the Toco Folk Museum for providing the information on which this report is based.

Comprehensive Exercise #4
Developing extensions of prototypical brands

The cost of building a major new consumer brand in the world's three main markets, the US, Japan and Europe, is estimated at $1 billion (Randall, 1997). Unfortunately, it is particularly difficult to cut these costs. One way of getting around this problem is through *brand leveraging*, which involves attaching established brand names to new products, as either a line extension (e.g. Diet Coke), brand extension (e.g. Jello Pudding Pops), or image transfer (e.g. Calvin Klein wristwatches). Using the brand name in this way can substantially reduce introductory costs and it can increase the probability of success (Aaker, 1990).

This strategy is difficult to employ for *prototypical brands* however; these are brands that so strongly represent their product categories that they have become almost generic terms. For example, consumers may well have lost sight of the fact that they are referring to brand names when they mention Kleenex, Band-Aid, Xerox, Saran Wrap, Teflon, Scotch-Tape, Rollerblades and so on. Extending such prototypical brands is problematic because the attributes of the original product may inadvertently be transmitted with the extension, and their strong core associations can limit new learning. For example, you may want to transmit the "softness" of Kleenex, but you may end up transmitting images of what Kleenex tissues are usually used for. Picture using Kleenex T-shirts as one would use Kleenex tissues! The association would not help sales of t-shirts.

Why is it so important to study such brands? Well, first of all, prototypicality is an important concept in consumer research. It has been found to be positively correlated with numerous aspects of consumer behaviour such as recall, learning, brand awareness and liking (Ward and Loken, 1988). Second, the markets for many of these prototypical products are mature, making it all the more important for these brands to be able to benefit from extensions.

So is it possible to use brand leveraging for prototypical brands? In a 1998 study entitled *Prototypical Brand Extensions: Not your Generic Marketing Strategy*, Robert Laufer, an MBA student researcher at Concordia University, found that prototypical brands, in certain categories, can in fact be successfully extended.

The author surveyed consumers about their opinions of hypothetical extensions. Using this information to test numerous hypotheses, the study found that the factors leading to favourable evaluations of prototypical brand extensions are not so far removed from those involved in "ordinary" brand extensions. For example, by far the most important predictors of extension success were found to be the overall fit between extension and parent categories, transferability of manufacturing skills, and positive evaluations of specific extension attributes.

The study also found that extension success was positively related to the consumers' ratings of how prototypical the product was, and their attitude toward parent brand. However, unlike the results found in previous research of non-prototypical brands, this study showed that extension success is negatively related to how difficult it would be to manufacture the extension category. In other words, the less difficult the manufacturing process, the more successful the extension of prototypical brands is expected to be.

Prototypical brand managers can use these results to predict the conditions under which favourable extension evaluations would occur. For example, the ideal brand extension would be a product that fits highly with the parent, involves the same skill set in manufacturing, and is in a category that is easy to manufacture. Marketers must also ensure that the extension has specific attributes that are desired in the new category. By following these recommendations, even prototypical brands can benefit from extensions.

Summarized by R. Laufer, MBA.

References:
Aaker, David A. "Consumer Evaluations of Brand Extensions," Business Review, Sep/Oct, 1997 pp. 135-143.
Laufer, Robert. "Prototypical Brand Extensions: Not your Generic Marketing Strategy," Concordia University Thesis, 1999.
Ward, James; Loken, Barbara (1988). "The Generality of Typicality Effects on Persuasion and Comparison: An Exploratory Test," in Advances in Consumer Research, Vol. 15, Michael J. Houston, ed. Provo, UT: Association in Consumer Research, pp. 55-61.

Comprehensive Exercise #5
Abuse of power in the classroom - toy company fights back!

NEW YORK, April 10 /CNW/ - FLICK-TRIX FINGER BIKES are currently the instigators of an enormous controversy that is raging within the classrooms and schoolyards of North America. These miniature die-cast BMX bikes - recently featured in USA Today and The Wall Street Journal as one of the strongest emerging trends in the entire toy industry - are today being sold in epic numbers. Reports throughout the country indicate that schoolteachers and several powerful educational bodies are in fact 'confiscating' these tiny collectibles. Unfortunately, this is not another case of teachers restricting distractions in the classroom. The current situation can only be described using those dreaded words...MASSIVE COVER-UP!

With the FLICK-TRIX frenzy in full effect, Spin Master Toys has sold over 5 million finger bikes. Where are these bikes today? Simply look in the desks and briefcases of teachers coast to coast. When solicited for comment, one teacher, who asked not to be named, said, "I thrive on being able to take the bikes from my students. I now have all of Series 1, and I just can't wait until Series 2 comes out." Others are being more discrete about their affinity for this new toy. Greg Lewis, business manager for the Dumas Texas School Board, would neither deny nor confirm the massive confiscation that occurred in his town just a few days ago. He did say, however, that the Finger Play phenomenon is an issue that cannot be overlooked any longer.

As the craze continues to grow, whispers from within the walls of Washington suggest that the United States Congress may soon intervene and control the use of FLICK-TRIX in schools, in order to prevent what, in their eyes, is an inevitable epidemic. Despite such rumors, Spin Master Toys continues to lead the way in the EXTREME SPORT world of toys. BMX extreme riders, Matt Hoffman, Fuzzy Hall, and John Purse action figures are in the process of being introduced into the market. Playsets are also on the way: bowls, platforms, and half-pipes combine to create over 50 different BMX parks. Perhaps the most anticipated launch is the FLICK-TRIX carrying case...that will give teachers the opportunity to collect 12 bikes in just one swoop!

As for the teachers and school boards across North America, Spin Master Toys' only public comment up to this point is, "HEY TEACHERS! LEAVE OUR KIDS ALONE!"

www.newswire.ca/releases/april2000/10/c1536.html
[Accessed 11 April 2000].

Answers to selected exercises

Exercise 2-1

1. *Claim: Loyalty between employees and firms does not exist any more.* The statement of the claim may not use these exact words, but the sentence should involve both the employees' loyalty to the company as well as the companies' loyalty to their employees. The indicator words "as a result" in the second to last sentence signal that a conclusion is upcoming (in the final two sentences). It should be reworded to make it a clear, stand-alone summary of the claim. This is a contestable claim.

3. *Claim: Children aged 9-14 have become an important target market for manufacturers and retailers.* The indicator words "there can be little doubt" signal a conclusion. The claim can be stated using the word "tweenies" instead of "children aged 9-14," but since the former is a jargon word which may not be understood independently of the text, it would be wise to avoid its use in the statement of the claim. This too is a contestable claim, despite the use of the words "there can be little doubt." Did you argue that the claim is unproblematic because the actions of manufacturers and retailers are verifiable facts? The difficulty with this argument is that these "facts" are not independent of interpretation. Words like "very successful and very lucrative" need to be justified and should not be accepted without question.

5. *Claim: Testing consumer products on animals must stop.* This is the first sentence of the paragraph which explicitly presents the author's thesis. It is a contestable claim. You may have strong beliefs that the claim is correct. If so, remember that a claim believed to be true can still be described as contestable. In other words, justification must be

provided; a simple statement of the claim is insufficient. Without evidence, claims like this run in to the dead-end of "My opinion against yours."

Exercise 2-2
The unproblematic claims are #3, 6 and 8. All the others are contestable and will need to be justified. Remember that you may be in full agreement with a claim, but it is still contestable.

Note: #7 is interesting because it is usually seen as an unproblematic, common sense state-ment. This unproblematic claim is made contestable, however, by Alfie Kohn in his 1993 *Harvard Business Review* article entitled "Punished by Rewards." Kohn argues that rewards do not differ much from punishment in that they are manipulative and create a workplace where people feel controlled. They make employees compete with one another and encour-age them to conceal their shortcomings from their supervisors. Rewards discourage risk-taking, learning and progress. Finally, psychological research shows that rewards actually undermine intrinsic interest in the job. Recipients come to see rewards almost like bribes; they perceive themselves as working because of the salient reward, rather than because of their own enthusiasm for the task.

In the same vein, Richard Farson (*Management of the Absurd*, 1996) believes that "praising people does not motivate them." Again, he argues that all evaluation makes us uncomfort-able, even positive evaluation. The person giving the praise is, by implication, standing in judgement over us. Moreover, praise is frequently used as a "sugar-coating" for reprimand. Parents and teachers are always using the "sandwich" technique which recommends that you say something nice before and after giving criticism. The result is that we have become conditioned to brace ourselves for reprimand whenever we hear praise.

Both these authors, then, provide us with reasons to label #7 as a contestable claim.

Exercise 3-1

Claim: Executive pay is too high, and this is decreasing employees' morale and productivity.

Evidence: Average pay increases and executive salaries in Canada; examples of highly-paid US executives, quote from an employee

Accuracy: Do you know any executives with salaries in the ranges described here? Do you have independent information about employees' reactions to high-salaried executives? Per-haps you have heard of employee complaints or union actions. If so, you will be able to judge the accuracy of the information here.

Precision: The salary figures given and the quote from the auto plant manager convey the sense that these averages were actually calculated and that the employee was actually interviewed. The precision of the evidence increases our confidence in its accuracy. An area in which precision could have been improved is in the evidence about salary freezes and layoffs.

Sufficiency: The evidence for high pay among executives may be sufficient, but just a single statement by one worker is not sufficient to convince us of the part of the claim that says that employees are upset by executive salaries. The author would need to present information from a larger number of people on this point.

Representativeness: Following the above, it would be good to get input from employees in a wide range of industries, not just the automotive industry. Perhaps the reaction is quite different in the "high-tech" world, for example. It would have been interesting, too, to hear from members of the board of directors of companies about their viewpoint.

Authority: The endorsement of the claim by Diane Francis of the *Financial Post* lends authority; the *Post* is a well-respected newspaper. Citing some scholarly research would have increased authoritativeness further. Again, a comment from a board member with expertise in the area of executive compensation and its effects on motivation could have been useful.

Clarity of expression: The claim was clearly stated and the evidence was presented in readable prose.

All in all, on the basis of your own assessment of concerns like those listed above, you would decide how persuaded you are by the text.

Exercise 3-3

Claim: Counterfeiting is a big problem that is poorly controlled.

Evidence: Estimates of the frequency of counterfeiting; counterfeit products can be dangerous; people believe that counterfeiting is a minor crime; the law is not adequately enforced.

Accuracy: You should think about whether you have any independent information about the existence or frequency of counterfeiting, or if you know of instances in which people overlook the problem of fakes, implying that the problem is "no big deal."

Precision: Numerical estimates are provided for the frequency of counterfeiting of music recordings, toys, watches, perfumes and software; these numbers probably could not be much more precise since measurement of illegal activities is difficult. The example of the one person who went to jail also lends precision to the argument. Precision would have been stronger if statistics had also been provided about the life-threatening fakes. Perhaps, too, a quote would emphasise the point that people have a lackadaisical attitude towards counterfeit merchandise.

Sufficiency: Four different pieces of evidence are provided which seems reasonable in a piece of this length. Since the author ends with a call for stricter government action, however, more evidence is needed to support the position that the government is just "going through the motions."

Representativeness: The types of evidence are moderately varied covering different industries as well as legal issues. It would have been nice to hear the point of view of manufacturers (legitimate or otherwise) or law enforcers, for example, for a fuller picture.

Authority: A primary source of information is the Financial Post, a well-respected magazine. The text also mentions that Pricewaterhouse-Coopers, a well-known consultant firm, collected some of the data reported here.

Clarity of expression: The claim could have been stated more clearly either at the start or the end of the piece, however, this was fairly simple to read and understand.

All in all, on the basis of your own assessment of concerns like those listed above, you would decide how persuaded you are by the text.

Exercise 3-5

1. Get Bank of Canada statistics on electronic fund transfers (EFT)
    Search for newspaper reports on the volume of e-commerce
    Interview firms who sell on the internet about the changing volume of electronic sales
    Survey a sample of consumers about their buying habits

3. Review the social work literature to find academic articles about the issue
    Conduct interviews with elderly people and their children or neighbours
    Interview doctors or psychologists who can provide expert views
    Talk to veterinarians and pet trainers who might have useful input

5. Get Statistics Canada information about immigration and emigration patterns
    Search for newspaper reports about the brain drain
    Ask a sample of human resource managers in large firms who hire frequently in "high-demand" areas

Exercise 4-1

3. Wives should ensure that their husbands are well dressed. Alternatively, spouses are responsible for each other's presentation.

5. Entrepreneurs owe it to their children to offer them jobs in the business. Alternatively, relatives should have priority for jobs in family businesses.

7. Chinese people know good Chinese food.

Exercise 4-2

1. **Claim**: Commercial advertising should be allowed in universities.
    Evidence: Senior administrators want funds from corporations; ads are everywhere; students and staff say they are not affected.

    Assumptions:
    Senior administrators should be the ones to make the decisions about accepting commercial advertisements. This may be a value assumption held by people who respect those in authority, or who think that senior administrators are best placed to see the "big picture" of university functioning. For these people, the evidence would be relevant. The evidence might be seen as irrelevant by people who believe that senior administrators do not spend a lot of time in classrooms or common areas and so might underestimate the impact of the ads. Such people might prefer the views of students or teachers who spend considerable time in the areas where the ads are located.

    The university is just one more place, like everywhere else, so it is okay that it has ads like everywhere else. The evidence is relevant. The alternate viewpoint is that the university, as a centre of education, is special. You would not expect to see commercial advertising in a church, temple or court room–the ideals of religious and legislative institutions are different. Similarly, the ideals of educational institutions make them special places. The presence of advertising on the streets and public transport vehicles is irrelevant.

    The presence of ads has no effect on people. If they are not distracting they should be allowed. On the other hand, it could be argued that people are often unaware of the effects of ads, so we cannot rely on their say-so that the ads are not problematic. For example, should we therefore feel free to expose our students to subliminal persuasion to get credit cards or expensive cars? Without knowing it, they (and we) could be wooed into debt.

3. **Claim**: Using the Internet to post jobs & resumés causes job-hopping.
    Evidence: 500 career sites on the Web; Frequent web searches by young job seekers; Easy access to job postings and resumes.

    Assumptions:

    Seeing a large number of jobs or resumes causes people to be dissatisfied with what they have presently. When people are made aware of a large number of opportunities they will be likely to find several other jobs that match their skill set. Some of these will probably have better starting salaries, vacation time, location, etc. so this will cause dissatisfaction with the current job. On the other hand, even if people see other job opportunities, they may realise that the benefits of moving are outweighed by the difficulties associated with relocating and getting settled in a new organisation. This will dampen feelings of dissatisfaction. Many people will realise that although another job looks good on paper, the grass often is not really greener when you are actually standing in the neighbour's back yard.

    Short tenure in a given job is undesirable. Firms need to more than 4-6 months before they can start getting value out of an employee. This is generally agreed on. Some might argue, however, that it depends on the type of job you are hiring for. For physical labour, simple tasks or short-term needs, short tenure might not be a problem.

    The writer is assuming that an *increased number of postings means increased use as a selection device.* This may be so, but perhaps firms are using the internet just because everyone else is. When it comes to hiring, however, they may prefer the old-fashioned techniques of referrals, university site visits, headhunters, etc. Thus increased postings may not result in more jobs being offered or more job-hopping.

    Young people who are looking for jobs will continue to use the internet to look for jobs as they get older. The person who holds this assumption may also believe that *as children reach job seeking age, they will continue to turn to the internet.* It is, however, difficult to predict technological advances, other than saying that there will continue to be "more of same." Unlikely though it may seem, the internet might well fall out of use in years to come, superseded by a new, more efficient technology.

5. **Claim**: Smokers who go against the advice of their doctors should be placed last on hospital waiting lists.
    Evidence: British doctors do this; the Canadian health system is over-extended.

    Assumptions:

    Doctors are authority figures who should be obeyed. People who value respect for authority would be likely to agree with this assumption. People who think individual freedom is more important would be less convinced.

Sick smokers who continue to smoke should be punished. Yet some people see smokers as victims themselves–tobacco companies are the real culprits because they have "hooked" people at a young age, and now these people find it extremely difficult to quit smoking.

The behaviour of British doctors and the British National Health Service are appropriate role models for Canadians. It may be countered that Canada should be setting their own priorities in managing health care, not just following the lead of another country.

If the system is over-extended, we should react by making lists of priorities. It can be argued, however, that more money and other resources should be put into the system, rather than just agreeing to make do with less.

Exercise 5-1 (Part I)

In general, the more diverse, plausible explanations you thought of, the better. Here is a sample of causal explanations that other students came up with.

1. You've overslept three times in the past week.
   I've been up late every night studying or partying with friends and I'm tired
   My alarm clock must need a new battery
   I may be coming down with a cold or something
   The seasons are changing and my body is reacting to changes in temperature, light or humidity
   There's something I have to do that I'm unconsciously avoiding
   This is an improvement–I usually oversleep every day

3. It takes you an hour to finish an exam that is scheduled to last for three hours.
   I studied hard and know my material well so I sailed through the exam
   The exam set was not long enough for the scheduled time
   I went too fast and carelessly because I was worried about time from the start
   I didn't know the answers to most of the questions
   The exam paper I got was missing the last three pages

5. Although overall industry sales are down, your product is exceeding projected sales figures.
   My product is superior to the competition
   My sales force is exceptionally good
   I underestimated my budget figures
   Marketing and advertising strategies have paid off
   My product is in a specific niche where the target market is growing relative to the population (e.g. seniors)
   My clientele is more faithful than average

7. You didn't get the promotion you feel you deserved.
   I've made mistakes I'm not aware of but my boss knows about them
   Company policy says no-one gets promoted before a year in a position and I've only been here six months
   Bad timing—I asked at a time when sales figures were down
   The company is being restructured and they are trying to flatten the hierarchy.
   Unfair preference was given to someone less deserving
   My expectations were unrealistic (e.g. I think everyone is stupid except me & I should be president)

9. One of your less talented subordinates is invited to lunch by your boss.
   The subordinate is going to be fired and they're doing it gently
   The boss being a mentor, helping the subordinate to improve
   The boss is attracted to the subordinate and is trying to develop a personal relationship
   They are already friends, unbeknownst to me, and they're just lunching together to enjoy each other's company
   The person is more talented that I realize and is going to be promoted

Exercise 5-2

1. **Claim:** The ban on cigarette smoking on air planes is causing the incidence of air rage to rise.
   The **causal explanation** offered: When passengers are deprived of nicotine they become stressed and this causes them to be violent and abusive.

   Rival causal explanation: Perhaps the author is correct, but perhaps this is an example of the *post-hoc fallacy* at work. Just because increases in air rage *followed* the cigarette ban, this does not mean it was necessarily *caused by* the cigarette ban.

   It is possible that media portrayals of road rage have caused a copycat effect on the air planes—it may have nothing to do with cigarettes. In general, we have witnessed an overall increase in reports of violence and anti-social behaviour (in schools, domestic abuse, etc.) so air rage may just be one more manifestation of a general problem. We also know that in recent years, more people are travelling by air and the level of service offered may be deteriorating. The weather in recent years has been more unpredictable as well (global warming?) and may be causing delayed flight schedules as well as flight turbulence, both of which upsets people.

   Many of these factors started having their effects at about the same time that the cigarette ban was put in place. Any one, or some combination of them might be causing air rage, independently of the cigarette ban.

3.   **Claim**: Having family-friendly policies makes firms more profitable.
     The **causal explanation** offered: Employees are happier and more focussed on their work, so they are more productive.

     Rival causal explanation: The author has explained the *difference between two types* of firms–those that have family-friendly policies and those that don't–by focussing on one possible difference between the two groups of employees. This explanation is quite plausible, but there may be other differences between the two types of firms that we should consider.

     For example, firms with family-friendly policies also tend to be large, established firms with human resource departments. Profitability, then, is explained by the size of the firm– large firms enjoy economies of scale, for example, and are generally more profitable than smaller firms. In this case, the feelings of the employees and their family concerns may be irrelevant. In other words, if size and family-friendly policies tend to go together, it is hard to tease apart which of these two factors may be causing profitability. It may even be both.

     It is also possible that profitable firms can afford to be more generous with their employees, offering them perks that are not possible for firms where budgets are tight. This explanation is akin to *reverse causality*; profitability precedes (and causes) family-friendly policies.

5.   **Claim**: Requiring board members to own large blocks of shares increases profitability and share prices.
     The **causal explanation** offered: Board members who own shares then have a financial interest in the company. They can be expected to do their best to ensure that the firm does well.

     Rival causal explanation: There is a correlation between the two variables and the author is assuming that one (share-ownership) is causing the other (share prices). The most plausible rival explanation is based on *reverse causation*, perhaps share prices are causing share-ownership. More specifically, it may be the case that when a company is doing well, the directors decide to buy shares.

     It may also be argued that when board members hold a significant number of shares, employees are aware of this and it increases their confidence in the organization. They are therefore motivated to work and their hard work will improve profitability. In this case *the direction of causality is the same* as the author proposes, but *the underlying explanation is different*.

7. **Claim**: Being referred by an insider increases your chances of being hired.
The **causal explanation** offered: Insiders can give you more information about the firm and the job, and this privileged information makes you more successful.

   Rival causal explanation: Here again, we have two groups of job applicants, those that are referred and those that are not. The author proposes that the referred group are given inside information which improves their chances. We must ask: Are there any other likely differences between these two groups?

   One such difference is that employees would be most likely to refer people whom they think would be competent. Suggesting the name of someone who turns out to be a poor performer reflects badly on the referee. Chances are, then, that the group of people who were referred had higher skills than the group who were not referred. After all, anybody can send a resume in to a bank, however good or bad their qualifications. Thus is may be the better qualifications of the referred group that led to an elevated hiring rate, and nothing at all to do with insider information.

Exercise 6-1

This exercise is something of a classic; variants of it are frequently used in class demonstrations. Did you find that the different people you talked to gave you very variable answers? What might be some of the reasons for this variability? Often it is because people of different ages and backgrounds have very different experiences which lead them to view the world through totally different lenses.

The exercise shows the importance of providing precise, concrete details in your writing. When you use vague words, the images people get in their heads can be quite unpredictable!

Here are some answers provided by a few people known to the author. Mr. P is a 60 year old accountant. Hannah is a high-school student aged 15. Barry is 20 and attends university, while Susan is a 47 year old teacher.

name	middle-aged	high-paying	large city	low-paying	small town
Mr. P	40	$50,000	500,000	$25,000	100,000
Hannah	40	$400,000	300,000	$45,000	10,000
Barry	38	$100,000	1 million	$30,000	30,000
Susan	45	$90,000	25 million	$15,000	1,500